SECRET LETTERS

A Battle of Britain Love Story

JOHN WILLIS

MENSCH PUBLISHING

Mensch Publishing
51 Northchurch Road, London N1 4EE, United Kingdom

First published in Great Britain 2020

A catalogue record for this book is available from the British Library

ISBN: HB: 978-1-912914-17-3; eBook: 978-1-912914-18-0

2 4 6 8 10 9 7 5 3 1

Typeset by Newgen KnowledgeWorks Pvt. Ltd., Chennai, India
Printed and bound in Great Britain by CPI Group (UK) Ltd,
Croydon CR0 4YY

MIX
Paper from responsible sources
FSC www.fsc.org FSC® C020471

To Odette
In memory of Ted, Audrey and Ken
Without whom

'... the Battle of France is over. I expect that the Battle of Britain is about to begin... The whole fury and might of the enemy must very soon be turned on us. Hitler knows that he will have to break us in this Island or lose the war. If we can stand up to him, all Europe may be free and the life of the world may move forward into broad, sunlit uplands. But if we fail, then the whole world, including the United States, including all that we have known and cared for, will sink into the abyss of a new Dark Age made more sinister, and perhaps more protracted, by the lights of perverted science... If the British Empire and its Commonwealth last for a thousand years, men will still say, "This was their finest hour."'

Winston Churchill
June 18 1940

AUTHOR'S NOTE

The letters of Pilot Officer Geoffrey Myers are not conventional. For a start, they were never posted, never dispatched to his wife, Margot, and his two young children, who were trapped in that part of France occupied by the Germans. The letters, in English, were written by hand in four small notebooks and start with the heading: SECRET. PRIVATE. They were to be read after the conflict and remain secret while the war was being fought. Whether he survived or not, Myers wanted his children, whom he hadn't seen for months, to know exactly what their father was experiencing as the brutal aerial war raged over southern England.

Myers was the intelligence officer attached to 257 Squadron in Fighter Command during the dramatic and dangerous days of the Battle of Britain. He was born into a Jewish family in Hampstead, North London, and had been a journalist for the *Daily Telegraph* before the war. At different times he was based in Berlin, just before the Nazis were beginning their ruthless rise to power, then London and Paris. As he wrote his letters, he had no idea if he would ever see his family again. In their hiding place in occupied France they were in constant danger of being arrested by the Nazis. Equally, as a Jewish journalist, now in the intelligence section of the RAF, Geoffrey himself would have been rounded up and killed had Hitler's invasion of Britain been successful.

The letters do not follow a neat, chronological structure through the Battle of Britain. In fact, they do not begin until September 8 1940, when the aerial war against the Luftwaffe had already been raging for several weeks. Geoffrey, it seems, had bottled up all his fears about his family trapped in occupied France, as well as the horrors of the Battle of Britain that he had already witnessed.

Eventually, the emotional dam burst and the words came pouring out. For days afterwards, almost in a stream of consciousness, he explained to his wife and family what had happened to 257 Squadron with a mixture of deep feeling and journalistic skill.

The letters zigzag backwards and forwards, starting with the Battle of Britain at its height then stepping back to Dunkirk, for example, and then back again to the middle of the Battle of Britain and then to its start. I have tried to keep faith with Geoff's intentions, but have occasionally reordered material to make more sense of it for the reader. If any of that does not work it is my responsibility, not Geoff's.

In addition, in common with many letters or memoirs written during the war, Myers changed names, even in the privacy of letters to his own family. This was presumably because he knew that one day his words would be read by outsiders, perhaps by accident. Geoff even gives himself a pseudonym, referring to himself as George in his notebooks. Flight Lieutenant Officer Hugh Beresford is called Allen and Flight Lieutenant Peter Brothers is named Eric Paisley. The legendary Squadron Leader, Robert Stanford Tuck, is dubbed Lucas and his unhappy predecessor, Squadron Leader Hill Harkness, is called Wight. To add to the secrecy, some pilots were given two pseudonyms; Carl Capon is both Capell and Masters, and Peter Blatchford is both Blackford and Fenley.

In the much more limited extracts I included in *Churchill's Few* (Michael Joseph, 1985), I also used a pseudonym for Squadron Leader Harkness – Sharp. This was because so much of the material is deeply critical of his behaviour, I did not feel comfortable with such public censure of an elderly man who was then still alive. Now, and in the updated edition of *Churchill's Few* (Mensch, 2020), I can use his correct name which, in the intervening years, other authors have put into the public domain.

I have changed names wherever I could to the real ones, and all the major participants in this narrative are identified by their true names. On a few occasions, when it has been difficult to be absolutely certain of a pilot's legal name, I have stuck with the pseudonyms given by Myers. At the same time I have, wherever possible, labelled geographical places correctly rather than by the initials used by Myers. So, for example, M is RAF Martlesham Heath and L is Lowestoft.

As the footnotes show I have used many other sources to add extra testimony and support to the letters of Geoff Myers. I was lucky enough to interview Geoff and several other 257 squadron members back in the early 1980s. More recently, the Myers family kindly gave me access to the short memoirs of their mother, Margot, translated from French by her daughter, Anne, as well as other fascinating material from the war.

As with all history, truths can be slippery. Even the Myers letters have a number of passages crossed out or changed. There is an occasional conflict between different sources or two contrasting recollections of the war. The chaos of scores of aircraft shooting at each other is a contributory factor to this, as is the natural desire to come out on the right side of history. As a virtually contemporaneous record from a respected journalist, I have given the letters of Geoffrey Myers significant weight.

No one can question the punctilious way that Myers did his job. In addition to Geoffrey, I met several members of 257 Squadron and read other accounts of events inside the squadron when I initially researched this period for *Churchill's Few*, and also more recently for this book. Everyone I met spoke of the integrity and conscientiousness of Geoffrey Myers and supported his record of the tragic events that befell 257.

The almost unique mix of personal and professional anxiety gives these secret letters an emotional charge and an intensity that is rare. Myers was reaching down into the very depths of his feelings to write with great frankness and openness. For him, after the war there was a constant tension between a wartime spent accumulating secrets and confidential information, and his training as a journalist which advocated a commitment to exposure and publication. I know that Geoff had been considering publication for some time before he gave me permission to use these letters back in the 1980s. His children, Robert, Anne and Bernard, have generously supported their father's wishes and let me see further unique notes and memories. They have also given me access to their father's original, handwritten notebooks which contain some differences to the typewritten copy I had received from him. Geoff believed that, eventually, these materials needed to be put on the public record and had already given the BBC access to some.

I only knew Geoff in the later stages of his life. We met in London and I took my young son to see him in Paris. My wife, Janet, spent some happy and stimulating hours interviewing his remarkable wife, Margot.

In these letters, Geoffrey Myers can be seen as serious, even severe. That is perhaps the effect of being a relatively older man attached to a squadron of young pilots who were facing probable death or injury on a daily basis during that summer of 1940. I find it hard to fully reconcile that with the Geoffrey Myers I knew. Small and darting, with wavy grey hair and twinkling eyes, Myers was warm and gentle. He cared very deeply about other people as well as the wider world, as his letters show, but he was also entertaining and fun. Those lighter characteristics, and his sense of absurdity, only creep into this correspondence from time to time.

I had enormous respect as well as affection for Geoff and felt honoured that he trusted me enough to permit me to publish his letters. Most memoirs of the Battle of Britain were written long after the war, with an inevitable risk of time dimming memory. Contemporaneous accounts of such a frank and intimate nature are extremely rare. Individual narratives on this scale, encompassing two of the great turning points of the war, the Battle of Britain and Dunkirk, and much else besides, just do not exist.

The letters from Geoffrey Myers to his family are unique, offering an original insight from a witness to so much history. More than that, the letters tell a powerful love story of two people caught up in war and at real risk of never seeing each other again. As their son Robert told me, his parents enjoyed a devoted marriage and so theirs was a love story that continued for the rest of their lives.

Now, the eightieth anniversary of that momentous instant in the history of this nation, with less than a handful of Battle of Britain pilots still alive, seems absolutely the right time to put their story on the record in a fuller and more detailed form.

Chapter One

September, 1940

Three months now, and I have kept silent. I have been hoping to write letters that would reach you. I have been wanting to do something that would help you to escape from Occupied France and to get us all out of this living grave. I haven't had the courage up to now to write letters to you like this, in a notebook, with the knowledge that you may never see them. My Duckies, you know without my writing that my thoughts are all the time with you. And yours are with me, my Lovvie. They bear me up.

These were the first words written by Pilot Officer Geoffrey Myers, intelligence officer attached to 257 Squadron, when he opened his notebook during the Battle of Britain to record scores of vivid and often intensely personal letters to his family. They were to be read after the war in the event that he never saw his wife and two children again. A disastrous day for his squadron in early September had finally propelled Myers into writing his experiences down.

We've all grown old since the Squadron was formed a few weeks ago. We've changed. It's grim.

By early September 1940, the Battle of Britain was close to its most intense. 257 Squadron, based then at RAF Northolt in West London, had been torn apart by a never-ending succession of deaths and injuries. Just a few days before his first letter was written, Geoffrey's anxiety had been heightened by Hitler's September 4 speech at a rally in Berlin in which he repeated his desire to invade England:

> 'In England they're filled with curiosity and keep asking, "Why doesn't he come?" Be calm. Be calm. He's coming! He's coming!'

Geoffrey Myers was born into a wealthy Jewish family in North London. In the 1920s, he was sent by his stockbroker father, Nathaniel, straight from his schooldays at University College School, in Hampstead, to Berlin to learn German. There, he managed to find a job as an office boy with the *Morning Post* and impressed everyone with his intelligent and conscientious approach to work. He was swiftly promoted to be the telephonist and then a subeditor.

Yet even in a cosmopolitan city like Berlin, with its cafe society and cultural progressiveness, Myers could see the early seeds of Nazism being sown as the country sought to recover its national pride, almost extinguished in the ashes of World War I and the ignominious peace that followed.

Geoffrey enjoyed his life in Berlin, attending concerts and parties, going canoeing or to the theatre. An elderly German-Jewish woman taught him the German language. Yet he was cautious about Germany and the Germans, especially as a Jew from England. He watched the looming post-war economic crisis emerge, and with it a lack of social and political cohesion. By the time he returned to England in 1931, where his father was ill and died soon after, he was clear; in Germany, Jews were becoming the enemy.

When Geoffrey returned home, he was pleased to be out of Germany. His work on the *Morning Post* and his knowledge of the country was impressive, and so he managed to land a job as a temporary sub-editor for the *Daily Telegraph*. He also enrolled on a Russian course at King's College, London. However, the worldwide economic depression put a sudden end both to his temporary job and his studies, and so, in 1932, he moved to Paris as a summer relief in the offices of the *Daily Telegraph*.

He soon met and fell in love with a nineteen-year-old music student called Marguerite Guimiot, who was a friend of his sister's. There was a difference in both age and life experience, but they were immediately happy together. Even Guimiot's strict mother was forced to admit that, though at twenty-seven Geoff was older than her daughter, as well as out of work and a British Jew, he was 'a very, very decent fellow.' Indeed, she thought that he was 'a feather in her daughter's cap.'[1]

In 1933, Geoffrey and Marguerite, or Margot as she was commonly called, were married, but Geoff was soon back in London working for the Jewish Telegraphic Agency. Margot stayed behind in Paris to finish her studies, and the newly wedded couple were only able to meet at weekends when they slept at Geoff's office in London or occasionally at his sister's flat in Gordon Square. Separation was hard for the two; so, in 1934, Geoffrey gave up his job and moved to Paris so that the newly-weds could be together. Fortunately, Geoff was

[1]Interview with Janet Willis

eventually able to return to the *Daily Telegraph* in Paris on another temporary contract, standing in for someone who was ill. The job uncertainty was frustrating but at least he and Margot could be together.

Geoffrey and Margot were soon settled and happy in pre-war Paris. Margot taught music and played in concerts, and Geoffrey finally secured a permanent job as a correspondent for the *Daily Telegraph* and also translated a book by the French writer, Jean Giono. The couple bought a flat where they lived with their two young children, Robert, born in 1936, and Anne, who arrived two years later. Only the dramatic changes in Germany, highlighted by the horrors of Kristallnacht in November 1938, posed a threat to their happy family life.

In Paris, the noises of impending war began to grow louder. Two of the weekly newspapers were openly anti-British and anti-Semitic. *Je suis partout* published special editions, *Les Juifs* (*The Jews*) and *Les Juifs et la France* (*The Jews in France*), which were full of racist propaganda. The arrival of many Jewish refugees from Germany stoked up further anger. Even Margot's previously liberal brother began to suggest that Hitler would bring order to the chaos of Europe.

Margot recalled, 'Geoff could see the war coming but I did not believe it was. I didn't want to think about it. I was absorbed in my own happiness: a husband I adored, two children who were my joy. I acted like an ostrich and hoped that Geoff would prove to be a poor prophet.'[2]

[2]Memoirs of Margot Myers translated by her daughter, Anne

Determined to defend freedom against the Nazis, Geoffrey hurried to the British embassy in Paris to volunteer. Training was merely a few days' drill in the embassy cellars with three other volunteers. A tailor was even sent over from Savile Row to measure the men for their uniforms.

In July 1939, the Myers family had a gentle holiday on the Isle of Wight. The tranquillity of the little island sat in stark contrast to the dramatic events taking place in Europe. Geoffrey recalled, 'I knew war was going to break out any moment. I just had to get back.'[3] Margot solemnly noted that they were virtually the only passengers on the boat heading to France.

Once he had volunteered, Geoffrey Myers was desperate to get into action, to be on the front line. Finally, the day before war broke out, the patience of Pilot Officer Geoffrey Myers, as he now was, was rewarded. He was dispatched to join two RAF squadrons at Berry-au-Bac near Guignicourt, north of Reims.

As soon as the war started and her husband joined the RAF, Margot Myers took her children south to the Guimiot family home at Lucenay-lès-Aix near Moulins, north of Vichy in central France. The house, Beaurepaire, was large and square, with a slate roof and large French windows. In the grounds sat a seventeenth-century timbered barn. The family home seemed as solid and safe a refuge as it had been for her father in the Great War. Margot remembered, 'I was naive about the political situation then. I never imagined that we would be overrun by the Nazis. I felt very safe in central France in the house I was born in. The house had been in the

[3]Interview with Author

family for nearly a hundred years. I lived there as a young child during the 1914–18 war. I imagined that this would be the same. I thought that this was the safest place in the world.'[4]

Her assumption was not unreasonable. Her grandfather had worked as a labourer on the farm at Beaurepaire, eventually buying it from the owner. He later showed his cleverness by also acquiring neighbouring farms. So Margot was surrounded by neighbours who were aunts, cousins and other relatives.

Moulins, on the River Allier, less than twenty kilometres from their home, was the border town between the two halves of France – the demarcation line. Margot and her children lived just inside the occupied zone where the Germans controlled every aspect of life. From Moulins, heading south, lay the unoccupied or free zone of France run by Marshal Pétain from headquarters in Vichy. Pétain was compliant, indeed complicit, with the Germans, and so the freedoms of the unoccupied zone were only relative.

By 1940, as the Battle of Britain started, Margot's family house had shifted from being a safe refuge to a dangerous trap. Although the solid house was buried deep in the Allier countryside, Geoff fully understood that his half-Jewish children could not survive the surrounding Nazi occupation for long.

Are you being harassed by the tricks of German propaganda, cursing their allies of yesterday? It won't make a difference to what you think, my Love, but it's terrible to be a prisoner in a mental cage.

[4]Interview with Janet Willis

He was desperate for his wife and children to escape, a plan full of danger. Geoffrey could not even send letters to his family in German-occupied France. It was just too risky. There were informers everywhere, happy to tell the Nazi authorities where children with Jewish blood might be hiding out.

The couple's only realistic hope of secure contact was through brief messages smuggled through friends in Clermont-Ferrand, the Renards, which was inside Free France. Geoffrey was wracked by worry for his young family in danger.

Soon I'll have the courage to take your photo out of my wallet and to look at my babies. I don't do it because it hurts too much. They can't destroy my faith and confidence. Whatever happens, I'll always trust you, My Luvvie. There is something that binds us together that's so strong that all the bombs in Europe can't smash it. You know you can trust me, Ducky, and that does me good.

Geoffrey was conscientious and professional and refused to let his anxiety for his family obstruct his crucial wartime job. As intelligence officer for one of Fighter Command's front-line squadrons in the Battle of Britain, Geoffrey Myers was close to the centre of the intense conflict on a daily basis. It was Geoff's job to observe, note, analyse and report all incidents involving 257 Squadron. This information was passed to 11 Group HQ of Fighter Command, based at Bentley Priory in London; a piece of the larger intelligence jigsaw needed to fight the Battle of Britain.

At one level this was a technical job but, with so many young pilots killed or injured in the first few weeks of conflict, Geoffrey was also desperately needed as an emotional support for those young men who were lucky enough to survive. It was also his melancholy duty to write to the families of those who had been killed. In his notebook he wrote:

September 8 1940

For the first few weeks after joining the Fighter Squadron as intelligence officer, I was like a living ghost. I knew it but, try as I might, I couldn't shake off the pall. I've done it now. I'm a normal human being again. I've taken myself in hand and stopped living in a bad dream.

The gloom was of no use to you, my Loves, and it was depressing for those around me… I can't help getting these day-nightmares about you all in German-occupied France. At first, they were such that I longed for the night, because although I had nightmares, they were as nothing compared with those of the day. But I've almost stamped them out. I'm calmer now and more useful again to the boys.

As the letters begin, the primary focus was not on his family but on the desperate plight of the Battle of Britain squadron to which he had been attached. Geoffrey Myers would look around the faces of the pilots, and they all seemed so very young.

Most of the boys had just finished their training. I suppose the youngest was about nineteen… I was struck by their youth, but they soon realised that I was not a Big Brother from Group HQ, but an uncle.

Geoff was thirty-four, almost twice the age of the youngest pilot, and the young flyers soon understood that Geoffrey was there to support them.

The squadron had originally been formed in Dundee in 1918 but was disbanded after less than a year. It was hastily re-formed over twenty years later, on May 17 1940, at RAF Hendon. It was also called Burma Squadron, because the Burmese people had helped to support the squadron financially. Translated from Burmese, their motto was 'Death or Glory'. As the operations record book (ORB) stated, 257 would have an establishment of one commanding officer, ten officer pilots and ten airmen pilots.

One of those airmen, newly arrived Sergeant Pilot Reg Nutter, observed that 'Most of the pilots joining the squadron had never been in a fighter squadron before, nor had they flown Spitfires.'[5]

So the pilots trained on the speedy Spitfires but, apart from their excitement for the sleekness of their new aircraft, the recently re-formed 257 made an uneasy entry into the war. On May 24, the ORB stated, 'There is still no ground equipment available, work going on with what we can borrow.' Just as bad, it reported a few days later that 'the maintenance units from which our aircraft have been delivered failed to wire them up properly,' and that the radio frequency was 'most unsatisfactory.' Never mind the urgent need for combat readiness, on May 26 it was reported that 257 'went to Church Parade this morning. Today is a National Day of Prayer.'[6]

The squadron had been drawn from far and wide. In terms of class, 257 ranged from the Honourable David Coke from Holkham Hall in Norfolk, son of the Earl of Leicester – the perfect image of the British aristocracy at war – through to sergeant pilots like Jock Girdwood, Bob Fraser and Ronnie Forward from working-class

[5]Battle of Britain Monument website
[6]National Archives, Kew

Scottish families. The three sergeants from Glasgow were the first men to arrive at 257 when it re-formed at RAF Hendon. Then there were university graduates like Alan Henderson, the sons of Britain's professional classes, and a sprinkling of pilots from the Commonwealth including Jimmy Cochrane and Camille Bonseigneur from Canada and John Chomley from South Africa.

Although they were a disparate, relatively inexperienced group, there were still some good pilots in 257. Flight Lieutenant Hugh Beresford had been transferred from Group HQ at Stanmore and was a little older than the others at twenty-four. He was given the leadership of A Flight and had both expertise and some leadership skills.

The difficult and disorganised start to the war continued for 257. On June 10 they were unexpectedly informed that the pilots were to be retrained on Hurricanes, instead of flying their beloved Spitfires. The next day, eight Spitfires were swiftly flown away to storage and eight Hurricanes arrived. On June 12 eight more Hurricanes arrived at RAF Hendon. The squadron was surprised and disappointed but, as one pilot optimistically pointed out to Myers, 'we can take it.'[7]

Roland Beamont from 87 Squadron summed up the strengths of the Hurricane, 'The Spitfire always looked like an elegant and beautiful aeroplane but I felt somehow that the Hurricane was more rugged. You got this immense feeling of power… it was very stable and it had a wide undercarriage which was very forgiving and it was not difficult to land.'[8] Sergeant Reg Nutter,

[7]Interview with Author, 1982

[8]Joshua Levine, *Forgotten Voices of the Blitz and the Battle of Britain* (Ebury, 2006)

from Hampshire, was one of the pilots in 257 forced to convert to Hurricanes. As the Battle of Britain Monument website records, he was less than impressed: 'I found it much heavier on the controls and far less responsive and somewhat slower than the Spitfire.'

Geoffrey Myers was fully aware of the dangers ahead, having been based as a journalist in Berlin before the war. 'I spoke German and had seen the rise of the Nazis. I saw them come into the Reichstag with their Heil Hitlers. The likelihood of invasion was obvious, to be followed by occupation. But the effect of Churchill's fighting speeches was incredible.'[9]

In June, Churchill said in one of his famous speeches, 'We shall defend our island, whatever the cost may be. We shall fight on the beaches, we shall fight on the landing grounds, we shall fight in the fields and in the streets, we shall fight in the hills; we shall never surrender.'

After the Battle for France, Fighter Command was in disarray, having lost scores of both aircraft and men. They needed to be replaced urgently. Money spent on building front-line aircraft for the RAF was dramatically increased to £55 million a week by June. Modest food rationing began. In early June, road and rail signs were obliterated and holiday beaches were covered with barbed wire to make any German invasion more difficult.

Myers was told in late June that 11 Group of Fighter Command needed the squadron to be operational on 1 July. According to the ORB compiled by Myers, the reply to Group stated that 257 would have twelve pilots operational within six weeks, by 16 August. Although

[9]Interview with Author

the lull after Dunkirk had given Fighter Command vital time to re-equip and regroup, 257 Squadron was still underprepared.

Geoffrey Myers instinctively knew, however, that the impending air battle was too urgent for his squadron's entry into the war to wait until mid-August. Sure enough, a few days later, on July 4 1940, 257 was moved from RAF Hendon to a more operational airfield at RAF Northolt in West London. All this movement and retraining did not help the young pilots. 'They were scarcely operational, these boys,' recalled Myers later.[10] They had never flown together before and had been hastily assembled with no squadron identity or history to fall back on. This meant that the role of squadron leader was more critical than it would have been for a more established squadron. Here, in the view of Myers, 257 was well placed.

For three weeks at the start of the Battle of Britain their squadron leader, David Bayne, relentlessly drilled his new unit in the skills of aerial combat. As Sergeant Reg Nutter observed, 'By the end of June, Squadron Leader Bayne had licked us into pretty good shape. We had all done a good deal of formation flying, air-to-ground firing and air-to-air firing.'[11] The operational records noted many hours of training, for example, 'individual crowd flying, oxygen climbs, air fighting as the programme of the day.'

David Bayne was, to Myers, the ideal squadron leader for a squadron that lacked cohesion, and where everyone was new to one another.

[10]Interview with Author, 1982
[11]Battle of Britain Monument

Just the sort of man we needed. Determined, conscientious and brave. Two years ago, he had a flying accident which left him with a wooden leg. You couldn't have guessed this, because he walked round with a stick and scarcely limped. That was the sort of man he was.

This single-minded man, with the eyes and chin of a hero, seemed destined to lead our squadron into battle and give it the inspiration of his own quiet courage. It was a happy squadron.

Bayne was vastly experienced and an exceptionally able pilot, with years of operational flying in Waziristan and on the North-West Frontier of then British India under his belt. But in 1935, Bayne had a serious accident when landing a Bristol Bulldog at RAF Duxford in Cambridgeshire on a very foggy night. He was badly injured, and this was how he had lost a leg. For two years he didn't fly but spent time in RAF hospitals and rehabilitation units, largely on half pay. But he was determined to be airborne again and, with a new wooden leg duly fitted, by 1937 he was flying fit once more.

Yet, despite his wide experience and the respect the pilots under his command had for him, Squadron Leader Bayne did not last long as an operational leader.

We were still stationed at Northolt when Bayne called the adjutant and me into his office. 'I have been promoted to Wing Commander,' he said. 'I shall be posted in a day or two.'

He got up from his chair and tripped ever so slightly over his wooden leg when making a greater effort than usual to walk smoothly. But nothing in his face betrayed his anger and dismay at being deprived of the leadership of the squadron just as it was becoming operational. He knew that he was being posted to a fighter control room

or below ground. He tried to talk casually to us about the squadron but his voice almost dried up.

Geoffrey Myers later added, 'Apart from using a walking stick he was otherwise completely normal. You could not wish for a better leader… it was disastrous for the squadron. David had built up a strong relationship with the men.'[12]

By July 20, a huge force of more than 2,600 German aircraft were spread along the coast of northern France. Hitler made plans for an invasion which was code-named Operation Sealion. The aim was for nine infantry divisions to land in Kent, Sussex and Dorset. By the time a third wave of forces landed, it was intended that 260,000 men would be ashore in Britain.

The next day, July 21, the day before he was due to be posted away, Squadron Leader Bayne did get his one chance to lead his unit into battle as the Luftwaffe gathered along the French coast. They were ordered down to the south coast to help protect a Channel convoy. Myers followed as a passenger and observer in a little two-seat Magister training plane.

As we flew down to the coast, I tried to dismiss from my thoughts the recommendation that the adjutant had made to me (about Bayne). 'Try to prevent him from doing more than his share… you know what he is, he will take on the Huns alone. He's only got today to do it. He'll be shot down! He'll be killed! My God! It's his last day!'

As they took off from their advance airfield, RAF Hawkinge, near the coast, even from his little observer plane well at the back, Myers almost immediately saw the enemy ahead.

[12]Interview with Author

They don't look as if they've scarcely completed their training. Nice formation! Bayne has them in hand. What's that? No ... yes it is ... it's an enemy formation flying in on them. I could recognise the Messerschmitt 109 fighters. Little black bastards. Bayne must have fired. He seems to be out of formation ... Bayne ... no must have been someone else ... stop flapping ... anyhow the Germans are halfway back to France ... France where the family is.

Despite his desire to end his only operational flight by shooting down some Luftwaffe planes, Squadron Leader David Bayne kept his discipline. His squadron did not engage the enemy, but stayed high above the convoy for eighty minutes as a protective shield.

I ran over to Bayne's plane. Anyway, it was my duty to take the report of the squadron leader first. 'Nothing to tell you,' Bayne said. 'They didn't come within range and we had orders not to leave the convoy. None of us fired.'

I knew what it had cost him in self-control to keep his squadron above the convoy. It might have been the great moment of his life. He was probably more experienced and a better shot than any of those German pilots who had almost come within range. There were clouds above the convoy. He might have left formation and made a swift attack. His squadron would have followed. He might have shot down two enemy planes... but he had orders and he knew they were sensible. His job was to stop our ships from being sunk. They were more precious to us than shooting down enemy planes.

We walked back together to our tent. He said nothing more. That night, back at Northolt, we gave him a farewell party in the mess. The next day, Bayne

assembled the whole squadron to announce that he had been posted. As usual, he had perfect control over his voice. Just a few words of encouragement and a smile.

Squadron Leader Bayne explained that the new squadron leader was Hill Harkness who had already been observing 257 Squadron for several days as a supernumerary. Harkness was a curious choice to replace a hardened combat leader like David Bayne, just at the moment that 257 was to be launched into the Battle of Britain as a front-line squadron. Born in Belfast, Harkness had been drafted in from the Flight Training School in Grantham where he had led a training squadron.

Geoffrey Myers was puzzled that a man so light on battle experience could be chosen to lead a wartime squadron, especially a newly formed one.

During those days when we were waiting for our first operational orders, Harkness was posted to us as an 'observer'. He seemed to be a misfit. Nobody took much notice of him. The adjutant and I were a bit worried about him being there. Anyhow, we felt sorry for him because he seemed like a lost sheep, so we gave him as much encouragement as we could.

Chapter Two

Having started to tell his wife about the Battle of Britain, Pilot Officer Geoffrey Myers's letters suddenly switch focus back in time to the Battle for France and Dunkirk, months before the Battle of Britain began. After all, Myers had not seen his wife and children since well before the evacuation of the British from Dunkirk and, even if this meant a diversion away from the urgent narrative of the events of autumn 1940, he wanted his family to know what his experience had been in France.

In the spring of 1939, Myers had been stationed at Berry-au-Bac near Guignicourt, north of Reims. It was a vivid contrast to the blood and horror that he was to see later. He was asked to use his French-speaking skills to requisition, for the officers, the local chateau which was owned by the Marquise de Nazelle.

The spacious and beautiful chateau became home to 120 men – eighty officers and forty batmen, cooks and waiters. The airfield nearby was in champagne country and that was the staple drink. It was more or less on tap and beer tankards overflowed with Veuve Clicquot. 'We went on consuming hundreds of bottles of champagne, popping off corks in the garden for target practice,' Geoff wrote to his grandson, Danny, many years after the war. To accompany the fizz, the wife of the local innkeeper kept the officers royally fed, despite initial resistance from the RAF cooks. Myers had arrived determined to learn everything he could about aircraft and gunnery but was soon appointed Mess Officer – and so ended up running what was, in effect, a grand hotel while he worked diligently from a small caravan in the next-door field.

One 12 Squadron member, Bill Simpson, recalled Myers. 'Geoff was regarded as middle-aged. He was intelligent, tolerant and convivial. He didn't seem to mind the youngsters pursuing the women of Reims... Geoff always had a lot to do; analysing intelligence reports, dealing with documents, sorting out language problems. He liaised between the French and the British.'[13]

As soon as her husband was sent to Guignicourt, Margot Myers and the children travelled down to what they thought was the safety of her family house in central France at Lucenay-lès-Aix. They joined her father, who had been a naval officer in the 1914–18 war and had returned home safely.

The married couple met once in Paris. Geoffrey's uniform, though tailored in Savile Row, was so baggy and large it made Margot roar with laughter. It was twice as large as Geoffrey and it was clear that the RAF had issued him with someone else's uniform. She immediately dispatched the shapeless outfit to a tailor in Paris for alterations.

Their second meeting, during what was later called the Phoney War, was in Guignicourt itself. It was strictly against RAF rules for outsiders to be there – indeed, Margot was not even supposed to know where her husband was posted – but one of Geoffrey's friends, an

[13]Interview with Janet Willis

American called Sam Jocelyn who lived in Guignicourt, smuggled her into the local hotel. Myers was concerned that Margot, who was pretending to be his niece, would be discovered, but for nearly three weeks Margot and their son Robert stayed out of sight in the hotel. From time to time, Geoffrey invited officers he liked and trusted to meet them.

When the family finally said a tearful goodbye, Myers had absolutely no idea when they would meet again. He could see that the RAF's defences, armed with old-fashioned aircraft like Battles and Blenheims, were flimsy against the might of a well-equipped Luftwaffe, battle-hardened in the Spanish Civil War. The pilots at Guignicourt called their Fairey Battle fighter-bombers 'flying coffins'. He was already fearing the worst.

After his family returned south, Myers was dispatched back to England to be trained at Hendon as an intelligence officer. He was pleased to be back in England, actually learning something that might be useful in the war, but his thoughts were often with his half-Jewish children in France. When his training at Hendon was completed, he was surprised to be sent back to France where he was attached to a section in Arras that dealt with photographic intelligence, mainly related to Holland and Belgium. He took up the story again in his letters to his family.

My love,

I have not told you what happened before I got back to England. I was immediately sent to Arras where I was attached to the intelligence section. At that time the only work being done in the section was photographic intelligence. My close companion there, Philip March,

refused to take the work seriously. Completely forgetting the task in hand, he would spend half an hour admiring the beauty of one or other of the photographs he was supposed to be classifying. When we had been working together for a couple of weeks he looked at me earnestly one morning and said, 'Your efficiency annoys and distresses me, Geoff. You should do the work with grand inefficiency as I do.'

But Philip March was not lazy. He just wanted to fight.

'Oh, why am I not fighting in Norway? I could get to grips with the Germans there instead of doing this nonsense.' March's jovial eyes and genial manner won for him many friends among the waitresses and hotel servants of Arras. He had a kind word for each of them, and always a good joke. They liked his handsome head of hair, his neat moustache and the panache which accompanied all his gestures. If it had not been for the war, March would have been riding over the fields of his Norfolk farm and writing about the yeomen of England.

'The trouble about England,' he said, 'is that we have forsaken the land. We are no longer of tough yeoman stock… It was the workman, the Cockney, the offspring of the peasant that won the last war for us… I think he is still tough enough to win this war, but if the town goes on sapping our strength, we shall not be capable of withstanding another onslaught.'

The section for photographic intelligence was run by a university lecturer called Belmonte, and his assistant had been a draughtsman before the war. They both had remarkable memories and a flare for interpreting photographs, but neither believed in basic classifying or filing.

In a special disorder of their own, both could find all the photos they wanted. Peter Crane, a young lieutenant, tried to put things in order but there was chaos. When he failed to persuade his chiefs to keep the section tidy, Peter lost most of his interest, finding instead plenty of amusement in the town after office hours. When Philip called him a licentious young man and teased him about his wife in England he listened indifferently.

The fourth member of the team was Paul, a French furniture dealer who had somehow talked his way into the section as an interpreter.

Paul was not usually communicative about his brothel experiences but he made up for this with a vengeance when he had had too much to drink. On these occasions, his eyeballs, which at all times protruded, appeared to stick right out and touch his thick glasses. Paul's particular assets were a magnificent American car and a thorough knowledge of all the restaurants, inns and cabarets in northern France. His contributions to the war effort were all in this sphere.

None of this jollity appeared to have touched Geoffrey Myers. He was a serious man, thoughtful and introspective. While the younger men still thought that war was a game or that nothing would ever happen to them, Myers, always the journalist, took a sharp interest in wider events. He seemed to carry the weight of the world on his shoulders.

I was billeted with a railwayman who had brought the sun with him from Rodez. The warmth of the south shone on his face. His dark hair was brushed straight back over his head. The sun of the south was also in his bushy eyebrows and in his dark, brown eyes. 'Just a little drop with us, Monsieur, before going up into that small room.' And he would bring out something dark and red, sweet and warming, which the family had brought back from South West France.

Madame Louis, the wife of the railwayman from Rodez, had survived the Great War in Arras and believed she would survive this one too.

Her father, a postman, had stayed at Arras after the authorities had ordered its evacuation. He had remained in his cellar when his house crumbled under the artillery pounding. He was the last man to move out of the town.

The railwayman's wife had great confidence in the Maginot Line and other French defences.

'We shall never see the Boche[14] here again,' she said. 'We shall keep him outside our Maginot Line and then we will show him, in his own country, what war is like. My friends advised me to send my belongings to Rodez and be ready to go down there. I did nothing of the kind. There will be no move this time. The Maginot Line... have you seen it, Monsieur? We saw bits of it on the films. Wonderful!'

Myers tried hard to gently prepare his landlady for the worst and, as a precaution, to send some possessions back south to Rodez.

'You know, I would not call it cowardly or anything like that if you were to send a trunk of belongings to Rodez, just a precaution against air warfare. It could do no harm just to send off a trunk...'

Madame Louis remained unmoved, her confidence in France unshaken.

[14]Shortened from French slang *alboche*, a portmanteau derived from *Allemand* (German) and *caboche* (cabbage)

That evening, I walked out of Arras and over the barren fields towards the river. In an enclosed field at the top of a gentle slope, I saw the signpost of the Imperial War Graves Commission. Hundreds of British soldiers had been buried there in a common grave. The grass had been allowed to grow. Poppies would soon be blowing their petals. Around the enclosure the ground had been tilled. I passed by and stumbled over a rusty shell which had been ploughed up and thrown on the path. Old shells were still exploding in unexpected places, sometimes killing small boys who played with them. Now we were at war again.

It looked peaceful enough there. A few miles away in the cafes of Arras, British soldiers were drinking Allies' beer, playing their mouth organs and singing 'Roll Out the Barrel' or 'Hang Out the Washing on the Siegfried Line'. Others were in the municipal theatre attending an all-British musical.

Officers were in the Café de l'Univers, passing away their time over gins and champagnes, reading war news out of the London newspapers which had been flown over by passenger mail plane to a peacetime schedule. Some complained when the newspapers were late.

As I walked on, the orange sunlight splashed over the clay-filled sand and gave a touch of richness to the barren uplands. I tripped down a little path towards the river. I came across a trench, which was overgrown and dated from the last war... at the bottom of the hill was another signpost pointing to Happy Valley Cemetery.

Soon after his peaceful but disturbing walk to the cemetery, Myers was told that a German invasion of Holland and Belgium was expected at any time.

Major Chase convoked us. He was a highly strung, conscientious man with a kind, understanding smile... He quietly told each man what his duties would be in the cellars of the Episcopal Palace where the emergency headquarters had been established.

At dawn the next day, May 10, Arras aerodrome was heavily bombed and at 6.30am the German invasion of Holland and Belgium was announced on Brussels Radio, as the Luftwaffe attacked scores of airfields. On the same day, Winston Churchill was appointed prime minister. The Battle for France had begun.

Pilot Officer Myers went to the palace cellars to sort out the intelligence photographs to find that only two of the many telephones worked, despite being tested every day. There, he was confronted by an unpleasant and lazy French officer nicknamed Monsieur le Comté who was abusive to his subordinates. Myers was pleased when he later met an altogether more admirable French lieutenant, fresh from fighting on the Maginot Line.

The lieutenant, who had a sense of values, remarked drily, 'Perhaps Monsieur le Comté will have to fight one day. Even the Maginot Line is not as comfortable as all that.'

Major Chase soon relayed to the other officers that the Belgians had failed to hold the line as planned. In the operations room in British military HQ, Geoffrey could see from the map of Belgium, with flags representing troop movements, that the Germans were advancing rapidly.

Day and night, weary old men, officers of the last war who had been called up from the reserve, pushed the flags deeper and deeper into Belgium. Signals came in with pathetic appeals from the British missions with the

French and Belgian forces for more aircraft to oppose the German onslaught.

A day later, the Germans had overrun most of Belgium and their tanks were pouring across Luxembourg into France. Our missions signalled that the allied troops were becoming demoralised by the incessant dive-bombing. Then came a signal that Brussels was in flames... the black lines and arrows showing the German advance were rubbed out and redrawn from hour to hour. Like ripples of the incoming tide approaching a child's sandcastle, they came, little by little, nearer to Arras. The signals from our missions became more desperate.

The Belgian defence was overcome in just seventeen days. In some ways, the war still seemed unreal. Rumours flew of German parachutists landing in Arras itself but no parachutes were seen. Every few hours, Myers and his fellow servicemen would surface from the basement for some fresh air.

Outside, the palace gardens were drenched in brilliant sunlight. The sky looked as if it had been painted blue. It seemed curious that such things as clouds could exist. We looked up to watch some planes circling high above the city. We imagined they were ours until a few anti-aircraft guns hurled up little white puffs around them.

Then came news that German tanks were sweeping along the road north of Reims, close to Guignicourt where, until recently, Geoffrey had been stationed. He immediately thought about the men and women he knew at the chateau near Guignicourt during the uneventful months of the Phoney War.

I thought of the villagers of Guignicourt who had grown to like the men of our two RAF squadrons stationed there during the Phoney War for the first eight months. A good

many of us had begun to feel quite at home there. Not long ago, the Mayor had shown me his orchard. 'Your pilots will enjoy the fruit this summer,' he'd said.

I thought of the innkeeper's wife who the airmen had called Grandma, who had taught the RAF cooks to make French dishes. I could imagine her gathering up her most precious belongings, hustling her elderly husband into their car and joining the stream of refugees moving south. I thought the inn had probably been reduced to ruins already, just as it had been smashed up by the German advance during the last war.

The ironmonger, who was called up months ago, was probably a prisoner of war by now. His wife and their four pretty daughters must have driven off in the ironmonger's van to a place of little safety. But the workers in the sugar beet factory had no cars and nowhere to go.

Geoff also thought of Madame Louis, the railwayman's wife, who had shown such faith in the strength of the French defences, 'I wonder what has happened to Madame Louis and those jolly little children of hers. I have the key to the front door. She had a trunk which contained my books and other belongings.'

Myers sat by his telephones waiting to pass on vital information, but the telephones did not ring. German tanks had crossed the Marne. He realised that all the phones had been cut off and that signals were the last remaining means of communication.

By dawn the next day, panic had seized the whole of northern France. The refugees were pouring through Arras on their way south. An unending stream of cars, with mattresses on their roofs, and packed out with worn-out women, frightened children and old men, was crowding along the road to the south.

Bill Simpson from 12 Squadron, who'd been stationed with Geoffrey Myers during the Phoney War in Guignicourt, recalled the horrendous escape from the airfield. 'The roads were chaotic, blocked by refugees. As we went along, we were strafed and bombed. The railways were full of cattle trucks and the wounded.'[15]

The German advance swiftly ripped through northern France reaching Arras by May 21. At British Headquarters the situation was chaotic and confusing.

Soon there was a regular flow of soldiers through the cellar passages to and from the car park. The stokers were handed piles of papers to burn. There were only two boilers. One was out of action… an urgent signal came through from the British Air Forces Headquarters to arrange for intensive bombing of the road to Bohain, along which a column of 200 German tanks was reported to be advancing. The British bombers were swiftly dispatched.

Half an hour later, after many frantic signals, it was revealed to Major Chase that the tanks were, in fact, French forces in retreat.

'It's too late. We've bombed them by now,' Major Chase said.

Stories of more bombs being dropped on Arras were flowing. Myers was asked go out onto the streets to try to establish what was happening.

In the town, all the streets were blocked with refugee traffic. Shopkeepers were hastily pulling down their shutters. Some had already left town. The salvage corps were removing from the streets the debris from the first bombing.

[15]Interview with Janet Willis

In the town, Myers saw the self-important French liaison officer who had been dubbed Monsieur le Comté.

He was perspiring with fear. He scarcely stopped to speak. He just shouted, 'We're off! We're off,' as he jumped into his car and disappeared with the French liaison officers.

Myers told the brave and determined French officer who had fought at the Maginot Line what he had seen.

'The cowards!' he said. 'One day they will remember this. France will make them remember. We are not like that.'

The main gates of the British HQ at the Episcopal Palace were locked when Myers returned.

Major Chase, who had scarcely slept since the German offensive began, seemed to have gathered every ounce of his nerve to carry on. His face became troubled as he thought for the first time of all the documents in the house up the road which had been our main office until the offensive began.

Myers volunteered to go back to retrieve or destroy the vital documents that had been left at the Intelligence Headquarters.

Before I left, I realised that I had not got a pistol so I borrowed one from a friend. I tried to think things out. 'If I get caught in the house,' I said to Major Chase, 'should I shoot myself?'

'I can't really advise you about that, Geoff,' he said.

I replied, 'I'm wondering what to do because I am a Jew and I don't know how things are.'

Major Chase said, 'Oh, that makes things different,' and he gave me a look of such kindness that I thanked him inwardly.

I decided that, if I was overtaken, I would try to shoot those who entered the house but not at myself. I told Major Chase. I also wrote down your name and address on a slip of paper and handed it to him in case he got out and anything happened to me. At the time I did not expect to get out of Arras and nor did he.

Chapter Three

The German advance had been frighteningly rapid. In the chaos that followed, Geoffrey Myers feared the worst. He could not see how he could possibly escape, trapped by the Germans on one side and the Channel on the other. But he had to just get on with the job at hand.

Major Chase had told Myers to remove or burn all the secret documents and photographs that were held at Intelligence HQ in Arras. When he arrived, three of his colleagues had already started the flames.

I went out into the blazing sun and made my way to our old office. There I found Belmonte, Peter and Paul sitting over a bottle of champagne, cursing the whole organisation of the general staff and wondering what was happening. In the back garden, a big bonfire was consuming air photographs and documents.

After some more burning of less essential documents it was decided that Paul, the Frenchman, would drive his car full of the most secret documents to a safe place further north. Myers, although reluctant to leave Arras, was ordered to accompany him.

A half an hour later we were winding in and out of streams of cars trying to find a way out of Arras to the south. Soon, we were alone going westwards on the road to Montreuil, near Boulogne. As we speeded through the still air, the smell of hay came in puffs through the

windows. I noticed a horse walking lazily in a meadow to some choice clump of grass. The dark green shadows of the trees on the glistening fields were becoming longer. The intense blue of the sky was softening. The setting sun dazzled Paul as he drove on. It was nightfall when we reached Montreuil.

The local French commander, a reserve captain who before the war had been a dentist, welcomed us like a monarch receiving royalty in his capital. He gave us a room for the night and helped us pile our documents into a cupboard. The next morning, he read us passages from both his diaries and his love poems. He was a stout little man with a big round head of closely cropped white hair. During his three months in Montreuil he had achieved his secret ambition: he had become a Napoleon. To assert his authority, he walked round with a riding whip which he frequently lashed against his breeches.

The dentist commander enjoyed this sense of power. He showed Geoffrey an old mill where hundreds of Belgian refugees were sheltering, and told him that 'the aged and the weak are being succoured by us... a beautiful sight.'

Everywhere (in Montreuil) there were broken-down cars and crowds around them, clamouring to push on southwards. Belgian generals, high Dutch officials, French industrialists jostled one another on the market square, crowded the small restaurants and fought at the petrol pumps to obtain a gallon or two of precious fuel. Lorries passed by with peasants and minor officials. Ambulances pulled up with wounded Belgians.

The restaurants ran out of food. The baker shops and grocery stores were emptied. The dusty trail of cars

with mattresses on their roofs passed on. The sun was relentless. 'The people of Montreuil are frightened at this sight,' said the Captain, 'but I have reassured them. While I am Commander of this town the Germans shall not enter.'

Finally, the afternoon after their arrival, the intelligence officers received a phone call ordering them to repack the secret documents into the car and drive immediately to Boulogne. Offices were swiftly found by Charles Belmonte in the Metropolis Hotel, and Myers and the other officers slept in an uninhabited house at the top of a hill. A lorry arrived and delivered all material still relevant to the intelligence section, even the camp bed belonging to Myers.

Boulogne then experienced the first of the bombings which, in the months to come, were to turn the harbour area into a shambles. German raiders sprinkled bombs on the lower town and then in our area. One bomb whistled down not far from the house and went into the ground with a dull thud. I woke up stiff with fright about five o'clock the next morning when the bomb exploded.

An hour or two after dawn an orderly came up from the harbour area to tell us that the Metropolis Hotel had been hit. A perfect piece of bombing had left a dark, jagged hole in the façade of the white building. That morning, news came through that German tanks had reached Abbeville, cutting off retreat from Boulogne to the south.

Command in Boulogne felt that the dangers of bombing had been overstated, but that is not what the Photographic Intelligence Unit thought. Their deputy leader, Charles Belmonte, said:

'If we don't get out before nightfall we'll all be in for it. Boulogne will be bombed to buggery.'

So, Belmonte arranged that they would move on to Wimereux. The documents were packed once again, this time into a lorry which headed for their new offices at the Picardy Hotel in Wimereux. Luckily, Belmonte found a nursing home in the town for the intelligence team to sleep in. It had already been evacuated and the doctor willingly handed the keys over to the RAF.

We tried to get supper in Wimereux but found nothing, so we motored to Boulogne and had a good meal in a restaurant by the harbour which was almost deserted since the air raids on the area had taken place. As we were finishing our meal the bombing began again. Peter walked quickly to the door, 'Come along. Let's clear out of here. Don't waste time. I'm off.'

That night at Wimereux, we watched Boulogne being bombed as we stood in our pyjamas on the terrace of the nursing home. After daylight, I was sent up to the Picardy Hotel and ordered to wait there for Charles Belmonte. I passed the time writing a letter to you and wondered whether it would be posted once the Germans caught up with us. I was interrupted by an air raid.

The men were ordered to destroy the rest of the documents apart from two cases of the most secret material. These were put in the charge of an officer who took them straight back to England in a destroyer.

'We saw him off,' Belmonte said, 'but for some minutes we doubted whether the destroyer would reach the open sea. The bastards went on plastering the whole harbour area, trying to hit her.'

When they could not find the keys to the remaining trunks, the small band of intelligence staff improvised.

Belmonte threw the trunks out of the window on the top floor of the Picardy and they flew open as they hit the ground. I turned the trunks on their sides with their backs to the sea and the lids open, screening them against the wind. Then we piled the papers up against them and set them alight. Soon, a roaring fire was consuming our records.

Peter found an abandoned staff car which the men pushed to get started, and Paul, the Frenchman, turned up in his immaculate American car. They had instructions to head for the coast at Dunkirk.

He [Paul] might have been a tourist. 'Did you see anything in Boulogne?' I asked. 'No, nothing special except the bombing,' he replied.

We spent the whole afternoon driving north-eastwards. I was in Peter's staff car with the gun I had picked up at the Picardy. The hapless refugees were now moving along the road in both directions. Thousands persisted in thinking they would find refuge by moving south. Others were returning northwards after finding they had been cut off by the German advance. Ploughs, tractors, prams and handcarts slowed down the traffic.

When cars broke down or ran out of petrol, they held up the painful procession for a few minutes before ruthlessly being pitched into a hedge or a ditch by those pressing on from behind. Most of the wanderers were too worn out to care but some still had terror in their eyes. They feared more machine gun attacks from low-flying planes.

Finally, the intelligence officers could make out Dunkirk ahead.

'Dunkirk appeared on the horizon like an ugly bit of black lace, but the black cloud above it across the sky did not seem natural. The cloud gradually changed into a huge serpent of smoke creeping above the factory chimney. It came from an oil tank which the German bombers had set on fire by a direct hit. Red flames were licking its tail. Peter looked at the smoke for a while, then turned to me. 'Filthy,' he said, and then kept quiet.

From Dunkirk, they were instructed to move five miles inland to Bergues. Myers was well aware that intelligence officers, men who most likely had never fired a gun, were a hindrance to a retreating army now.

A high staff officer, probably a respected member of some civilian profession less than a year ago, sat in his car with his pet dog and golf clubs… the headquarters was being established [by him] as if for at least six months. We went about billeting as if the enemy were hundreds of miles away… the apprehension which filled the town was oppressive.

The next day all our telephone communications were cut off. About fifteen planes had dive-bombed the town of Cassel, wrecking the telephone exchange, the post office and most of the houses on one side of the marketplace. The townspeople were removing the dead on improvised stretchers.

Two peasants were dragging a frightened, middle-aged man through the marketplace while angry women were shouting, 'Kill him! Kill him!' The man beseeched them in broken French to let him go, saying he was innocent. Others cried, 'Take no notice of him! Kill him! He's a German spy. He signalled to the bombers.'

Luckily for the man, the intelligence officers intervened before he could be killed by the crowd.

We stopped them from lynching a 'German Spy'. He was a German, indeed. He had fled Berlin from the Nazi persecution and had established himself in Brussels where he continued to teach oriental languages. We grabbed him from the crowd, took him back to Bergues and handed him over to the gendarmes there.

In the early hours of the morning, the men were all woken to be told that German tanks were close by.

I felt like a rat in a trap. So did the others. Unarmed men feel silly facing tanks. The German tanks were fifteen miles away and we had two hundred clerks, batmen and waiters with a few dozen rifles to defend us.

Some of the officers advised an immediate retreat to Dunkirk. Others insisted that we should stand and defend Bergues. They shouted at one another. Nobody was in command.

Fortunately for him, Geoffrey escaped the chaos and confusion when he and the other men from his section were yet again given new orders. On May 26 1940, Myers and Peter were sent on a drive into Poperinghe in Belgium with a secret message to be delivered to the colonel in Ypres.

Poperinghe was swarming with Belgian soldiers wandering about aimlessly, waiting for something to happen. We made our way through the crowds and drove on. Refugees were camping on the roadside. Peter delivered the secret message to the colonel, who told him it was pointless.

The drive into Belgium had been a waste of time, the secret message valueless, but at least they had escaped the chaos at Bergues and, in Belgium, there were no tanks to be seen.

When we returned to Bergues we found that makeshift defences had been put up. Ploughs and farm carts had been thrown across the roads. An odd assortment of British and French soldiers were on the lookout with cocked rifles at cottage windows.

In Bergues, Myers and Peter heard news of their former colleague in the intelligence section, Philip March, who had finally got his wish to fight. Near Bergues, his reconnaissance unit lorry had run into a column of German tanks. They were ordered out of the lorry by the Germans.

As they were scattering, another burst of machine gun fire came from the first tank. Philip, who had remained in the lorry until all the men had jumped out, must have been mortally hit. He fell off the lorry onto the road.

Also on their arrival at Bergues Myers discovered, to his horror, that Charles Belmonte and the rest of the intelligence unit had already left.

We were told that all non-combatants had been moved to Dunkirk. We were given orders to go immediately to Dunkirk. Without any sign of the enemy, we drove along the road bordering the canal, almost as if on an excursion. By contrast, Dunkirk was being dive-bombed when we arrived. The dock area was already in ruins. The red flames seemed to lick up the soot around the great cloud of smoke.

From the air, the sight of Dunkirk was disturbing as the American pilot, Flight Lieutenant Jimmy Davies from 79 Squadron, observed. 'The smoke from the innumerable fires in Dunkirk and the other French coast towns was terrific... A fellow pilot described it as being like a gigantic piece of cotton wool lying right across the

seashore as far as he could see, even from two or three miles up.'[16]

Raids had become such a routine that the French port officials looked at our papers impassively while the place was being bombed. By a freak of nature, a local thunderstorm burst over the port during the bombing. Our car got stuck in the debris. Under torrents of rain, we tried to push it out of a hole. We got it moving again and Peter drove to the quay where a destroyer was moored in readiness to take off for England with the rest of our unit.

We dumped the car and ran up the destroyer's gangway just before it was lifted. Four minutes later we left for England.

This was the last destroyer to leave Dunkirk. The rest of the massive evacuation was by fishing vessels and other little boats. All told, 243 ships were sunk in the evacuation and 68,000 people were killed.

On arrival at Dover, all on board were seen off the destroyer by a policeman whose routine had not changed since the cross-Channel services had been stopped. People were enjoying a warm spell. Some were sauntering along the jetty after a bathe. The only soldiers about were those who had already returned from France. Not far away, people were playing tennis. We had come from another world.

Geoff was attached to RAF Hawkinge for a few days to take reports from pilots about the evacuation at Dunkirk.

[16]Jonathan Reeve, *Battle of Britain Voices* (Amberley, 2015)

Above Folkestone, a few white lines of chalk showed up the scattered trenches and gun pits in the Downs around Hawkinge Aerodrome. Thinking of what I had left behind on the other side of the Channel I looked around uneasily, hoping to find some indication that our Channel coast was defended. There were none.

After his dramatic and fortunate escape on the last destroyer to leave France, one of 330,000 military personnel evacuated from Dunkirk, the thoughts of Geoffrey Myers were never far away from his wife and family, hiding deep in rural France. Communication was impossible with Margot and she had no idea that Geoff had made a dramatic escape from Dunkirk. But what would have happened to them if he had not made it safely out of France?

Then Myers's notes turn back to the battle for supremacy in the air.

I was sent to Hendon as intelligence officer in our fighter squadron which was being formed to fly out to the Cherbourg Peninsula, where it was thought we would hold a bridgehead. But we were soon engulfed in the Battle of Britain.

Chapter Four

The first days for 257 Squadron under their new leadership were spent at RAF Northolt. The uncertain start to the Battle of Britain had continued with the change of squadron leader. For some of the pilots it was difficult to get used to the new approach of Squadron Leader Hill Harkness, after the strategies they'd been taught by his predecessor. The words of one pilot, spoken on the day David Bayne had been replaced by Harkness, echoed in the head of Geoffrey Myers.

Sergeant Pilot Conroy, a chatterer, told us later that as Bayne walked away, he thought he heard him mutter under his breath in despair, 'And God help you all.' And I am beginning to think he was right.

So from the start, Myers was cautious about the new boss, especially given the outstanding leadership skills shown by Bayne. Nonetheless, he believed that concerns about Harkness would fade over time as the squadron got to know their new leader and vice versa. Fortunately, the first few days of August brought little action for 257 Squadron, just routine patrols, so there was a chance for Harkness and his squadron to develop an understanding of how to work together, without the pressure of endless scrambles and dogfights.

Light relief was provided for Pilot Officer David Coke, Pilot Officer Carl Capon and Sergeant Pilot Reg

Nutter when they were drafted onto VIP escort duties. In early August they escorted the Prime Minister, Winston Churchill, from RAF Hendon to North Coates, Manby and Coltishall before returning to Hendon. Churchill flew in a de Havilland Flamingo piloted by Flight Lieutenant Blenner-Hassett. Reg Nutter recalled, 'This trip remains vivid in my memory as the Prime Minister persuaded Blenner-Hassett to do some very low flying, for his benefit, across the Wash.'[17]

Only a few of the men in 257 Squadron were married. They were largely separated from their wives, who stayed at home in England, although Margot Myers was of course trapped in her remote home in German-occupied France.

As an exception, Pilot Officer David Hunt's wife of just a few weeks, Terry, moved round the country with her husband's different postings with the squadron. That is why her 1942 memoir *Pilot's Wife's Tale* was subtitled, *the diary of a camp-follower.* Writing under the name of Esther Terry Wright, she described how she regularly waited anxiously at RAF Northolt for her new husband to return. She watched the pilots coming into land through a telescope she poked out of the window in their rented room near the airfield, *'I watched through the telescope the sudden blur of a plane coming into range, too near to be in focus, big and flat and grey and barely opaque, and the port-light liquid red against the thin mist that was creeping over from the far side of the field... then there was a roar in the sky and David was over the roof, and home: a*

[17]Battle of Britain Monument. The operations record book has PO Chomley, not Capon, as one of the escorts.

flashing of recognition-lights, and a shock in the air after him.'

On August 8 1940, the days of escort duties and routine patrols came to a shuddering end. A large fleet, CW9 code-named Peewit, consisting of about twenty-five merchant ships, set off as a Channel convoy. It was the Luftwaffe's job to destroy the convoy and the Fighter Command's task to defend Britain's merchant ships.

From France, the Germans sent up fifty-seven Ju 87 Stuka bombers to attack CW9 near the Isle of Wight. They were supported by fifty fighters.

The day was a disaster for 257 from the start. Squadron Leader Harkness refused to fly, which was, to Myers, an extraordinary decision at this first critical moment for his unit.

There had been a mess up at the start from Hendon. Harkness stayed in his room, said it was his day off. Jimmy Cochrane, who had been drinking with the adjutant until four in the morning, did not wake up until someone called him a second time at nine o'clock. He was a bit put out when he was told that the squadron had pushed off to the south coast ... they were ordered right up into a blitz.

The first British plane to reach the enemy was flown by Flight Lieutenant Noel Hall, commanding A Flight of 257 Squadron. For the next twenty minutes, the sky was dark with planes in combat. Some of the pilots from 257 wondered what was going on; they had never encountered such ferocity.

That day, their first of serious aerial combat, three 257 pilots were shot down: Flight Lieutenant Noel Hall, Flying Officer D'Arcy Irvine and Sergeant Kenneth

Smith. The pilots were all killed within a frenzied few minutes around noon. In return, the squadron had one victory – an Me 109 was shot down by Pilot Officer Kenneth Gundry. Overall, the RAF lost thirteen pilots that day with three men severely injured. Of CW9's more than twenty ships, only four survived the brutal attack from a hundred German aircraft.

To cap it all, 257's two Flights lost contact with each other at a vital time in the combat. Lancelot Mitchell, a twenty-four year old from Scotland who was acting in charge of B Flight in the absence of Squadron Leader Harkness, had left his colleagues in A Flight vulnerable when he and his section charged off towards France.

Noel Hall led the squadron, but Mitchell suddenly left him and dashed off with his section towards France. I still don't know what possessed Mitchell that day. He told me afterwards, 'I can't think what happened. I must have misunderstood the vectoring.'

There were recriminations all round after a day of chaos and deaths, some of them avoidable. When the pilots failed to return, Mitchell and the late-rising Jimmy Cochrane, both consumed by guilt, flew back out again to search for them.

When they came back Mitchell looked at me blankly. 'I saw nothing,' he said, 'just the rest of our convoy the Germans had bombed, two ships on fire and a raft with dead men on it. No sign of Hall or D'Arcy Irvine. No sign of Sergeant Smith.'

The British convoy had been smashed. From the sky the pilots could see the Channel full of debris and men clinging desperately to life rafts, as they tried to avoid the burning oil that swirled beneath the thick black smoke from the burning ships.

Jimmy Cochrane tried to atone for being late by catching up with his colleagues and sticking the battle out to the very end. Indeed, he claimed an Me 109 destroyed but that, and any other successes for the squadron, were totally overshadowed by the horror of losing three colleagues in their very first blitz. The guilt Jimmy Cochrane felt was heightened by seeing Brian D'Arcy Irvine shot down right in front of him.

Cochrane was in a bad way. He felt guilty about his lateness and that drinking business, but he saw the end of the action. 'Poor D'Arcy boy. He yelled out to me over the RT [radio transmitter] "There's a Gerry on your tail," and they must have got him at that moment. I swung round, got on the tail of the Gerry and beetled after him. I'm buggered the Gerry didn't go splosh in the drink. Never been so surprised in all my life. He just dived and disappeared. All there was left was a big splosh of foam without me firing a shot at him.'

Brian D'Arcy Irvine was just twenty-two. He was a talented sketcher of birds and planes and had been tutored by his friend, the famous naturalist Peter Scott. Before the war he had studied architecture at Trinity College, Cambridge, where he was also a member of the Air Squadron. Irvine had used his artistic flair to create a camouflage scheme intended to confuse German air gunners as to which direction a Hurricane was actually flying in.

Geoffrey Myers had the unenviable job of finding the right words to say in letters to parents or partners of the dead pilots.

D'Arcy Irvine, always ready with a new scheme to improve the squadron, always keen. One of the best. I tried to write of D'Arcy Irvine as a hero to his parents,

but all the time I seemed to see him grinning over my shoulder. I could hear him saying, 'Looks all right that sob stuff, but a fat lot of use it is to anyone. Damn silly waste of a pilot, and then you write pretty letters about it. Well, I suppose you're trying to do your job.'

Sergeant Kenneth Smith was one of the airmen attached to 257. He was a popular young man, born in Bromley in Kent, 'one of the lads'[18] as a fellow sergeant pilot put it. Smith was twenty-one.

Soon after his death, Nazi propagandist Lord Haw-Haw broadcast Smith's name and address, and claimed he was now a prisoner of war. As a result, his mother kept his room untouched for many years in the false hope that he would one day return home.

Flight Lieutenant Noel Hall had joined 257 as a Flight Commander at Hendon in early June and, after a short spell away, had rejoined them on July 27 1940. The son of an admiral, Hall was a regular, with several years of flying experience under his belt. Born in Hampshire but educated in South Africa, he was a small, dapper man with wavy hair who was always immaculately turned out. He was shot down by Me 109s while defending convoy CW9 over St Catherine's Point. The loss of such a superior and experienced officer in their first major combat was a serious blow to the squadron. Hall was one of the senior pilots who could have filled the leadership vacuum created by the puzzling behaviour of Squadron Leader Harkness.

Noel Hall's body was recovered by the Germans and he was buried as an unknown airman. It was not until 1948, a full three years after the war ended, that his

[18]Ronnie Forward, Interview with Author 1981

cigarette case with his initials, a watch and a gold cufflink were identified by his father, and he was finally laid to rest in a marked grave in Criel Cemetery in France.

Lancelot Mitchell was distraught about his role in the disastrous events of the day. Exactly why he flew off in the wrong direction was unclear but given the scale and ferocity of the combat and the lack of leadership, it was not completely surprising. In any event, Mitchell had stepped up unexpectedly into a leadership role when Harkness had refused, not that Squadron Leader Harkness was in a forgiving mood.

We tried to make a loophole for Mitchell, talked of the difficulties in catching the vector over the RT, but Harkness wouldn't hear of that. 'It's just bloody rot,' Harkness shouted at Mitchell, in front of all the young pilots. This from a squadron leader who had not been up in the air in the first real emergency. 'You simply made off like a damned fool instead of following your leader.' That – coming from Harkness! I could have hit him.

That night, Myers went to see Mitchell, who was desperately upset.

Mitchell was cut up as it was. He talked to me for a long time that night. I wasn't sharing a room with him then, but I went in just because I knew he wanted to talk to me. 'I never let poor Hall down before,' he kept on saying. 'I'll admit it was my fault.' He looked haggard. 'This is a dog's life. I sometimes think I shouldn't have been a pilot at all.'

Not all the pilots of 257 were sympathetic to Lancelot Mitchell, as Myers recorded of Camille Bonseigneur, one of the Canadians.

Bonseigneur was the most unaffected chap you could imagine. He was small with rather a haunted look and

a little light brown moustache. 'Bonseigneur never shot a line,' Cochrane said very recently, 'he thinks too much for that.' Bonseigneur felt very deeply about everything that went on in the squadron. For nearly a week after Hall disappeared he refused to talk to Mitchell. 'Hall would have been our Flight Commander,' he said, 'if Mitchell had not been yellow.'

It was of no use telling Bonseigneur that Mitchell had a brainstorm and had flown off on a tangent. He scoffed at the explanation, but I knew it was the right one.

To the pilots of the bedraggled 257 Squadron, Hill Harkness had already committed the cardinal sin of refusing to fly in the squadron's biggest action of the war so far. As one sergeant pilot, Ronnie Forward, put it, 'He used to hide away somewhere. I don't think he led us at all. He didn't inspire us and he didn't always fly with us.'[19]

Myers was deeply concerned about how quickly his squadron was falling apart with three young pilots already dead. In the shadows of the evening, when he wrote his letters to his family, the anxiety of what was happening during the day only heightened the emotion of what he wrote down in his notebook at night, as he thought of the house in the country near Lucenay-lès-Aix where his family hid.

As the conflict unfolded, Margot and Myers realised they had probably made a mistake when they decided that Margot and the children should stay in France. Through smuggled messages from friends or via his journalist contacts, Myers heard of increasing Nazi activity in the area where his family was hiding. He knew from his pre-war years in Berlin that round-ups

[19]Interview with Author

of Jews and deportations to camps, or worse, would be the next step for the German-occupying forces. He took some comfort in the enduring nature of the landscape.

I get the sudden terrors when I think about you and the babies but I will not let them get the better of me. You would be ashamed of me. They have not interned you, Darling. I hope you are able to bear up. What have they done with the crops? They can't destroy the rivulet or the lovely shape of those gentle hills. They can cut down the oaks, they can empty the barns of their stocks and they can take away the poultry. They can persecute you, my Ducky. They could take you away from the children, destroy their souls. My God. I believe they are human, as we are human, but I have terrors. I pray for you my beloved and for my little children. We are fighting for hope, and as long as we are fighting, hope cannot be destroyed.

Trapped in France, Margot Myers had no idea whether her husband was dead or alive. Months after the evacuation from Dunkirk she received a letter that had been posted in England weeks before. It told her that Geoff had been on the beaches at Dunkirk but had just managed to escape. She was relieved that he was alive, but the letter was so old Margot had no idea what was happening to her husband in the Battle of Britain.

Although he could write down his most personal and tender feelings during the night, by day Myers needed to be alert and strong and not let his emotions hinder his work.

The catastrophic start to the Battle of Britain for 257 Squadron did not let up. Monday August 12 was a fine and clear day. Such was the unreality of the war for some of the nation that, on that particular day, twenty-seven people wrote to *The Times* about hearing a cuckoo call.

The Luftwaffe had more serious matters on its mind. The Germans' strategy was to precision target key radar installations in Sussex and Kent, followed by attacks on airfields on the south coast. Just four days after losing three pilots over the channel, 257 Squadron lost another man, John Chomley, a former sergeant pilot. Young and fresh-faced, with soft brown hair, Chomley had been flying one of the fifty-odd planes sent to defend Portsmouth from a massive German raid when he was shot down and killed. Squadron Leader Harkness and Flight Lieutenant Beresford both claimed 'probables'[20] that day but, once again, any success was blotted out by the loss of a pilot.

John Chomley had been with 257, his first squadron, for just over a month. He was only twenty years old.

Chomley and I got friendly. He had spent most of his life in Durban and his people were still in South Africa. He took me up in the Maggie [Magister training aircraft] when I chased after the squadron to be with them at the advanced airfield and take their combat reports when they landed. The job usually fell to new pilots... When we went home that night he shot up a friend in a little Sussex village, just clearing the trees as he dived down to greet her and then swooped up again. Two days later he disappeared in a blitz. I can't help thinking at times that he's still with the squadron and will walk into the mess with D'Arcy Irvine, Hall and the others.

A second 257 pilot, the Honourable David Coke, was shot down in the same raid that morning and

[20]Enemy aircraft pilots believed they had 'probably' shot down

had a finger amputated at the Royal Naval Hospital, putting him out of action until much later in the Battle of Britain. Coke was the son of the Earl of Leicester of Holkham Hall in Norfolk and godson of the previous king, Edward VIII. Like John Chomley, Coke was a popular colleague. Terry Hunt recalled, 'He was very good-looking and charming. He had a terrible stammer which miraculously disappeared when he was flying.'[21]

The squadron's cause was not helped by some inadequate equipment, particularly radios. Sergeant Pilot Reg Nutter recalled, 'I am sure that many early casualties were caused by the inability of pilots to communicate with one another quickly and clearly. I can remember being at the rear of the squadron with Pilot Officer Capon when we were jumped by Me 109s over the south coast. I attempted to warn him of one on his tail but, on talking to him later after he bailed out, I found my transmission had not reached his ears.'[22]

After the horrors of August 8 and August 12, the next few days, despite a strong increase in intense action from the Germans, were relatively uneventful for 257 Squadron. But on August 15, one of the young pilots in Myers's squadron, Pilot Officer Charles Frizzell was forced to bail out over London when the engine of his Hurricane caught fire. Frizzell remembered, 'Smoke and flame began to spew out from the protruding exhaust on both sides of the fuselage just ahead of the cockpit. With no power, I began to glide towards the rooftops of London below. Anxiously searching for an open space, I could find none.'[23]

[21]Interview with Author, 1981
[22]Battle of Britain Monument
[23]Letter to a collector of memorabilia, April 29 1977, copied to Author

He decided to bail out with his parachute from about 800 feet. 'I managed to land near a see-saw in the playground of an establishment called St. John's Orphanage, just off Edgware Road. I suffered not a single bruise. I began to be approached by some people who appeared to be anything but friendly. The reason was that, my name being what it was, I had painted in large, block letters across the back of my Mae West [life jacket] my nickname FRITZ. Once I had convinced the natives that I was not one of "them" everything changed. I was welcomed into the orphanage for a cup of tea.'

It was a close enough call for Frizzell to take a stark and unromantic view of aerial combat. 'Unlike a commando who has to do it with a knife, the fighter pilot was well insulated from the harsh realities of his action. He didn't get splashed by blood, hear the squeals or see the mutilated remains of his victim. It is in fact a nasty brutal little business.'[24]

On August 18, 257 Squadron moved out of Northolt to RAF Martlesham Heath, near Woodbridge in Suffolk. Perhaps it was an attempt to ease them back from the aerial front line over the home counties and to enable them to regroup. Martlesham Heath was one of the most northerly aerodromes in 11 Group of Fighter Command, but was well placed to defend both the east coast and the Thames Estuary.

However, the move away from Northolt did not signal an improvement in fortunes for the ragged squadron. On their first day at RAF Martlesham Heath, they were immediately sent to their forward base at RAF Debden, near Saffron Walden in Essex.

[24]Letter to Author, March 20 1982

With Harkness rapidly losing the confidence of the squadron, much of the responsibility and the strain of leadership fell on the shoulders of Hugh Beresford, flight lieutenant in charge of A Flight. A vicar's son from the small village of Hoby in Leicestershire, Beresford had joined the RAF straight from school, somewhat against the wishes of his father. At the beginning of the war he had married the nineteen-year-old daughter of an RAF officer. They had been married for just over ten months when 257 moved to Suffolk. The move away from London did not diminish Beresford's deep anxiety about the lack of leadership, as Myers reported in a letter to his wife.

'Harkness makes me tired,' Beresford said. 'I just can't stand the way he frigs about in the air every time there is a blitz on. We all shout at him that he's not following the vectors given by the controller, but it makes no difference. He just goes the wrong way then circles round and round in the air until the section leaders peel off and leave him.'

One of the Sergeant Pilots in 257, Ronnie Forward from Glasgow, explained the crisis in the squadron simply. 'I would say that morale was not at its highest… there was no leadership.'[25]

Pilot Officer Alan Henderson was blunter. 'Harkness would lead us away from possible action. He was also completely useless over the RT. Morale was terrible.'[26]

Geoffrey Myers was a sharp observer of human behaviour and had no doubt about the intense pressure Hugh Beresford was under.

[25]Interview with Author
[26]Interview with Author

Beresford had a nervous flicker in his eyes which might have made a man doubt his personal courage if he did not know him. There were no doubts about Beresford for the pilots in his section, though. He knew the risks but he did the job properly every time. If there is no leadership it costs lives. Pilots were killed through no fault of their own.

Chapter Five

Geoffrey Myers recognised that Squadron Leader Harkness was doing his best but was just not up to the job. His tolerance had limits, however, because the arrogance shown by Harkness was more difficult to forgive. 'Harkness did not realise what was happening. He was egocentric and self-centred.'[27]

Harkness was unwilling to listen to advice or ideas from the rest of the squadron, often shouting at anyone who disagreed with him. Pilot Officer Alan Henderson, a graduate of Jesus College, Cambridge, was upset that Harkness sometimes led his squadron away from the action; but Henderson was even more shocked to realise there were embryonic signs of defiance, even mutiny, among the unit. 'Some of the sergeants were talking about running away. I tried to cheer them up.'[28]

A short pause in their flying in August also gave the pilots of 257 more time to contemplate their own mortality. As Henderson put it, 'Anyone who says he was not frightened in the Battle of Britain is either a liar or an idiot. One of the best reasons for choosing to be a fighter pilot was that you were only shit-scared for forty minutes at a time. The other was that we were kings

[27]Interview with Author, 1981
[28]Interview with Author, 1980

of everything. Girls were flinging themselves at you all the time.'

For the wives of the tiny number of men who were married, life was not easy either. The women wanted some semblance of normal married life but, in addition to their continuing worries about the safety of their husbands, the men were endlessly moved round the country from one RAF base to the next.

Being a newly married wife of a Battle of Britain pilot was unreal and difficult, as Terry Hunt outlined in her 1942 book. Her dream of living with her husband in their own little house seemed impossible – and as 257 moved from Hendon, then to Northolt, Debden and on to Martlesham Heath in Suffolk, she moved from rented room to rented room. Meanwhile, David had been banned from staying off the aerodrome with his new wife.

'David had telephoned me about a fortnight before our wedding to say that his CO had warned him that children would result; and that David would not be able to live out until the war was over.'[29]

As Terry could not live with her husband, she moved back home with her mother. *'We lived quietly together, Mother and I, while David led his outlandish life. From 3.30 every morning to 11.30 every night there were terrible telephone conversations to and fro, when neither of us heard a word; or I would gather only that he was out of socks; and buying those and sending them off would make something to do.'*

Myers was sympathetic, even if Harkness was not. Clearly, Terry Hunt appreciated him, particularly when

[29]Esther Terry Wright, *Pilot's Wife's Tale* (Bodley Head, 1942)

Myers defied orders to ensure the newly-weds could actually meet. *'And then there was a message from the admirable Geoff, the intelligence officer, whose wife was in France with their baby. Geoff said it would be quite in order for me to come over and join David. It seemed a bold undertaking with the area banned and things beginning to happen at last.'*

So Terry Hunt moved into a room in a house facing the aerodrome. Terry watched the planes take off and land, always looking for her husband. *'I saw David and the others fly away one late afternoon. From the road I had watched David himself climb; and I had seen them all go and grow small in the sky.'*

Although the squadron leader had banned David from leaving the aerodrome, the rule was not being strictly enforced and so, with encouragement from Myers – who no doubt empathised and felt the pain of separation from his own wife – the Hunts had some semblance of a married life. *'It was a delightful and terrifying life. David would spend his last energy coming over to the house, washing perfunctorily in cold water, and falling into bed. We had no alarm clock. I would get into bed too and, with David already asleep, prop myself upright against the wooden rails of the bed and watch the dark and the searchlights away over the aerodrome. There was his breathing, an occasional plane engine roaring, when the plane itself might soar like a ghost across the window. There might be a bomb or two away in the distance. Time barely moved: certainly, it was not to be measured.'*

August 18 was a critical juncture in the Battle of Britain. Fighter Command had already lost more than one hundred pilots in the previous nine days and were significantly below strength overall, though not as threadbare as the Germans imagined. But the rate of losses was too high to sustain for long. Although Squadron Leader Harkness led 257 Squadron into combat that day, it was Hugh Beresford and his section who managed to get through the fighter escorts to attack the Luftwaffe bombers. Beresford himself hit a Heinkel 111.

Sergeant Alexander 'Jock' Girdwood, Beresford's number two, joined in the attack and also hit the bomber. Jock described the scene. 'As I broke away, bullets entered my cockpit which exploded and caught fire. After a struggle I managed to bail out and as I fell I succeeded in pulling the ripcord and in untwisting the lines which wound round my legs. After that, I was nearly strangled by the lines which got entangled round my neck. A toe of my right foot was fractured by a bolt which was forced into it by a bullet.'[30] He successfully crash-landed on Foulness Island not far from the destroyed Heinkel, whose pilot later died. Girdwood was taken to Foulness Hospital – and 257 Squadron was another pilot down.

As if in response to the terrible losses already suffered by the young pilots of Fighter Command, Winston Churchill made his famous, rousing speech on August 20. He thanked the British airmen 'who, undaunted by odds, unwearied in their constant challenge and mortal danger, are turning the tide of the world war by their prowess and by their devotion. Never in the field of human conflict was so much owed by so many to so few.'

The next week was relatively quiet, full of patrols and escort duties rather than more intensive combat, but

[30]Alfred Price, *The Hardest Day* (Macdonald and Jane's, 1979)

with 257 at full 'readiness' on most days. Flying Officer Lancelot Mitchell was still able to claim a Dornier 215 during this period.

On August 26 at 3.30pm the Luftwaffe mounted a huge raid of forty Dornier bombers on RAF Hornchurch and also RAF Debden, the forward base of 257 Squadron, where their groundcrew was stationed.

Women's Auxiliary Air Force (WAAF) Corporal Daphne Wallis, who had joined up aged seventeen, described taking shelter. 'In August we had a really bad bombing raid. We had all been given a shelter number but if you were on duty in the Ops Block you stayed at your post. As far as I can remember, some of the shelters did not have tops on them and my number was for one such trench. We had to jump in very fast, bearing in mind that the enemy was already dropping their bombs. I remember a girl jumping right on top of me and can still remember her name. We were devastated when the raid was over, so much damage, huge craters everywhere.'[31]

Daphne Wallis was lucky. Three 257 aircraftsmen, Underhill, Holmes and Collier, were killed as they took cover in a shelter trench. Myers recorded in his official file, 'Squadron Leader Harkness and Flying Officer Bolton had narrow escapes in the same shelter. Bolton helped in salvage work. Apart from the three dead airmen, several buildings were damaged and a plane destroyed. The three sticks of bombs which were dropped made tracks running from east to west. A bomb fell between the second and first hangar in which 257 Squadron had its headquarters.'[32]

[31]Battle of Britain Monument
[32]National Archives, Kew

Wendy Walker, niece of Aircraftsman Second Class Sid Collier, recounted that her uncle 'had been in the Air Force a few weeks when he was killed in a raid at Debden. As the attack took place, Sid and his friend ran to a shelter which was hit and collapsed on them, killing them instantly.'[33]

Sergeant Pilot Reg Nutter recalled, 'It is funny how things stick in one's memory but I remember that the sergeants' mess at Debden had a grand piano. The only one I ever saw in an NCO's mess, but the last time I saw it, just after the bombing, it was trying to hold up the concrete roof!'[34]

In his notebook, Myers described the horror of the bombing raid.

Holmes did not understand what we were fighting for. He was one of the three RAF clerks blown to bits when a bomb was dropped on Debden. He knew nothing about the war, regarded it as the weather, as something that happened.

One of the three dead men was married.

The wise old adj wrote to his widow saying what a fine chap he was. 'Luckily', he told me, 'I noticed that not all his letters were from his wife, but from a mistress of his in London. I burned the lot. His wife will be able to talk about her dear, faithful husband.'

Bolton, this morning over breakfast, couldn't think of anything better to say than to describe in detail how he dug out bits of Holmes and the other men who were blown to pieces... he relished describing the whole

[33]Wendy Walker, WW2 People's War: BBC History. WW2 People's War is an online archive of wartime memories contributed by members of the public and gathered by the BBC. The archive can be found at bbc.co.uk/ww2peopleswar
[34]Battle of Britain Monument

thing. 'We couldn't find one of the heads,' he said as a grand finale.

As August wore on, Flight Lieutenant Beresford's frustration with Squadron Leader Harkness had turned into anger.

Beresford would come back to the subject most on his mind. 'Why does Harkness just go into his tent after a blitz and read Men Only instead of talking things over with the other fellows? Why doesn't he attempt to lead them? Why does he even refuse to get on with all the administrative work that a CO must do? He might at least make up a bit by going on some of the dull convoy patrols. But he simply disappears into his tent and goes to sleep while the boys are wearing themselves out. When they make mistakes he just bawls them out with bursts of short-tempered abuse like a turkey.

Hugh Beresford had an aristocratic bearing although, in fact, he was a vicar's son. His father had been the Vicar of Hoby and Rotherby in Leicestershire for twenty-eight years. Some of the sergeants called him 'Blue Blood Beresford' because he was strict and serious. To his sister, Pamela, he was just a normal young man. 'Hugh did not feel he had any vocation... he liked to play cricket, kick a ball around. He had a rifle and a gun. The air force seems to have fascinated him.'

Myers said, 'I thought he was a good man. He took his responsibilities seriously. If anybody should have been squadron leader, it was Hugh Beresford.'[35]

The officers largely agreed. As Pilot Officer Alan Henderson put it, 'Beresford was a very nice chap. He

[35]Interview with Author

wasn't a line-shooter, but friendly with a sense of humour. He was a complete gentleman, friendly to everyone.'[36]

As the days of adversity piled up, he became a bit fidgety on the ground, but he remained brave and cool-headed in the air. 'Do you think there'll be a blitz tomorrow Geoff?' he would ask me. 'Look at the weather! What's the time?' A few minutes later he would look out and repeat, 'I'm sure there'll be a blitz. What's the time?' Sometimes he would ask that question four or five times in a quarter of an hour. The strain under which he was living penetrated my system, and I could do nothing for him. It was tough.

On August 31, British radar reported 200 German planes airborne and heading across the Channel. 257 Squadron, led that day by Hugh Beresford again, was one of thirteen squadrons ordered into the air. After they left Martlesham Heath that morning they engaged the enemy over Clacton at 18,000 feet. Both flight commanders, Hugh Beresford and Lancelot Mitchell, claimed Me 110s destroyed. Terry Hunt wrote that at the aerodrome '*a beaming man said that my husband had just called in after shooting down a plane and was pleased with himself.*' So was Pilot Officer Alan Henderson, who shot down two Me 110s himself. For a moment it seemed as if the tide had turned for 257 but, as ever, good fortune did not last.

Alan Henderson, something of a playboy with a queue of women chasing him, did not have long to savour his downing of enemy aircraft. Keen to add more hits to his tally, he singled out another German target and fired.

[36]Interview with Author

The next thing he knew, his own small fuel tank had been hit. 'The cockpit was full of flames. I've never been so terrified in my life. There was a smell of cordite. With a superhuman effort I opened the canopy and jumped out.'[37] The parachute seemed to take a long time to open and, when it did, the jerk was so fierce that it dislocated his shoulder. Henderson recalled, 'I drifted out to sea. I thought, Christ, I'm going to drown.'

Fortunately, a motorboat already carrying several German pilots pulled him out of the water. To his astonishment, one of the men who had come to his rescue was his peacetime stockbroker. Alan Henderson was still alive but he was another 257 pilot whose part in the Battle of Britain was over.

On that same day, Pilot Officer Gerry Maffett – a relation of the Harmsworth family who had worked on the family newspaper, the *Daily Mail* – was killed. Outnumbered four to one in the aerial battle, Maffett's plane was hit and then crashed at Walton-on-the-Naze. It was concluded that his parachute failed to open and he had died on landing. Alternatively, the Hurricane may have been at too low an altitude before Maffett tried to open the parachute.

Only a few days earlier, Maffett had written to his parents about a moment of glory when he claimed a Dornier 215:

> 'I attacked him from above and dived down on him. The intelligence people have given me the aircraft as shot down, as there was quite a glow in the fuselage as I dived away. I suggested that the

[37]Interview with Author

glow might have been the sun but they think he was destroyed. The Hurricane certainly is a grand aircraft.'[38]

That evening, Myers counted up the 257 squadron casualties so far. Since Harkness had become their squadron leader in late July, they had been engaged in about half a dozen major battles with the enemy. Despite the relatively small number of serious combats, the human cost had been high. Myers recorded the tally in the OPR. '257 Squadron result up to the end of August were nine enemy aircraft destroyed. Squadron losses F/L Hall, F/O D'Arcy Irvine, Sgt Smith, P/O Chomley, P/O Maffett, killed or missing. P/O Coke, Sgt Girdwood, P/O Henderson wounded. Sgt Forward sent for a rest after suffering shock. Eight Hurricanes destroyed. Three damaged.' [39] These fatalities listed did not include the three RAF ground staff killed in the bombing raid on Debden.

Pilot Officer Charles Frizzell summed up their vulnerability. 'The German fighters were tactically very smart and experienced... their tactic was to wait high on the perch a few thousand feet above their bombers and then, like Tennyson's eagle, who "watches from his mountain walls and like a thunderbolt he falls," would swoop down on some unsuspecting Spitfire or Hurricane... It was a form of back-stabbing. When we had the chance, we did the same thing. This was the case with D'Arcy Irvine, Hall, Fraser and the others from 257 – all stabbed in the back.'[40]

[38]Winston G. Ramsey, ed., *Battle of Britain Then and Now* (Battle of Britain Prints, 1980)
[39]National Archives, Kew
[40]Letter to Geoff Rayner, July 28 1981, copied to Author

Only a few days earlier, one August evening after 257 Squadron had moved to Martlesham Heath, David and Terry Hunt had held a small party to celebrate his twenty-third birthday. His wife, Terry, later wrote:

> *'There were eight pilots at the party and Geoff, the intelligence officer… after three weeks no one was in commission. David and I made a list. It was too complete to be shocking. It was perfect in its completeness.'*

Terry Hunt found herself next to a stranger. *'[It was] the same squadron leader who had tried to wreck our own married life by keeping David in like a child; and so we had plenty to say and I was charmed, and it was only when we were driving home that David had told me where I had expended my own charm.'*

In fact, Terry had been conversing with Hugh Beresford, who was not squadron leader but had enforced the decision of Hill Harkness to separate the couple. *'I never met him. Darkness they called him. He told David, "If you marry, you'll soon be popping out babies and won't be able to live in." I didn't like him for that.'*[41]

Of course, Beresford was the de facto Squadron Leader in the vacuum created by the inadequacy of Harkness.

Myers noticed the intense strain on the other senior pilot in the squadron, Lancelot Mitchell. After Hall's death on August 8, Mitchell had been promoted to Acting Flight Lieutenant in charge of B Flight, despite

[41]Interview with Author

being at fault when the squadron was separated and Hall and two others were killed. He now shared a room with Myers, who was surprised by a sudden rise in Mitchell's confidence.

He even appeared to be overconfident. He began to feel he was a virtuoso in the air. So he was, at aerobatics. When one flew with him, one felt him pass through the element like a bird. Every movement was natural and graceful. In the little Maggie, sitting in front of me, he would hedge-hop between the trees and above the cottages, skim up the hills and glide down the valleys with unbounded elation.

Yet underneath all this bravado, Myers saw the stress and tension.

The life of perpetual readiness, the strain of the air battles and the heavy odds had begun to tell on Mitchell. He had become fidgety and his big brown eyes would not come to rest.

In central France Margot Myers, despite her piano player's hands, worked the farm at Beaurepaire hard, hoeing beets or bringing in the cows. The outdoor work brought some peace to her anxious mind. 'I savoured enormously the silence and solitude of the fields. Yes, I savoured all this in spite of the anguishing news of the war, in spite of my worrying about Geoff.'[42]

One day Margot heard that a Dutch ship had been sunk by the Germans, 'She vowed never to board a ship with her children as long as we were at war. She could not guess what lay ahead!'[43]

[42]Memoirs of Margot Myers translated by her daughter, Anne
[43]Memoirs of Robert Myers with his sister, Anne

The house at Beaurepaire, with a small old house in its grounds, was swiftly full up, 'People who could began to flee the big cities. We were lucky to be at Beaurepaire. Many family friends began arriving. My grandmother took them all in. The house was full to bursting, sleeping in all rooms, including the attic.[44]

Margot, her mother and grandmother housed not just friends and family but some of the increasing stream of refugees passing through, many from Paris but from elsewhere too, escapees. She took in a mother and her four children who had arrived on a lorry. The family lived in the old house for several months before heading back to Paris. Then a man, his wife and nephew arrived on a little horse and cart. They had travelled all the way from Belgium like this. They, too, stayed for a time and the nephew worked on the farm attached to the house at Beaurepaire. But as the German grip in the area tightened, the Belgians moved on. Margot remembered, 'They were good people. Soon it was our turn. The rout had begun. Refugees blocked the roads, airplanes were shooting on civilians with machine guns and the French army were helpless. It was hell. We were aware of the German advance but had no idea of the magnitude of the disaster.'[45]

The prison in the border town of Moulins, La Mal Coiffée, which was housed in a fourteenth-century tower of what had once been the castle of the Dukes of Bourbon, had already received its first male internee. In August the first female internee was incarcerated there. At its height, it was to house nearly 500 prisoners,

[44]Memoirs of Margot Myers translated by her daughter, Anne
[45]Memoirs of Margot Myers translated by her daughter, Anne

mainly Jews and resistance fighters, primarily within its three floors of dungeons below ground. Margot Myers had good reason to be frightened.

In late August, Geoffrey Myers began to send coded letters to his family in France. He was aware of the increased level of German propaganda, including the broadcasts of Lord Haw-Haw. 'We were told that Britain was finished but I was absolutely confident that we were going to win,' said Myers. 'But I also knew that the atmosphere in occupied France was very difficult and I was afraid that my family might be denounced. So I couldn't afford to wait.'[46]

Geoffrey discovered that letters could be sent through Thomas Cooks for half a crown. They were open letters with no envelope, just a sheet of paper. Cooks said they would try to get these letters through to occupied France but that they couldn't guarantee success.

So Myers sent anodyne letters through to his wife and children in the name of his mother, using a code agreed between Margot and Geoffrey before the war. The first coded letter said, 'If you can get over here it is all right.' But Myers had no idea if the letter ever reached his family, and so he continued to write his secret letters into his notebook.

[46]Interview with Author

Chapter Six

At Martlesham Heath, David Hunt and Terry did not live close enough to the aerodrome for her to use her trusty telescope to watch over her husband landing safely. So, Terry took to waiting at the gate for his return in the evenings. *'Once it was dark, it was better than my room with its black-hooded light like an old-fashioned train. Tonight I had Mother with me. We looked at the immense sky, and the cage the searchlights made, closing us in almost. We agreed about their beauty.'*

September came, and RAF Debden was subjected to another mass bombing when 160 bombs were dropped. This time there were no casualties. Two days later there were more losses for 257 Squadron. Under the command of Hill Harkness, the squadron was in combat with enemy raiders over Chelmsford.

Pilot Officer Camille Robespierre Bonseigneur, the 22-year-old Canadian, was hit. He had been employed briefly in a car dealership in Canada before working a passage for himself over to England with the aim of joining the RAF. That day, 257 Squadron was scrambled too late to help stop the Luftwaffe bombing North Weald Airfield in Essex – and 257 only met the might of the German Air Force on their way home. Bonseigneur, flying P3578, was killed in an act of either bravery or foolishness. His death hit another young pilot Cardale 'Carl' Capon particularly hard.

He [Capon] said to me, 'We could do nothing against those planes that kept swooping down on us. They were flashing above the sky above us at 25,000 feet. There must have been hundreds of them. And Bonseigneur, the fool, just climbed up there into them, followed by me alone. Well, it was too damn silly. He was asking for it. Now he's gone and what's left of the squadron?' The strain was too much for him.

Bonseigneur was remembered kindly by Pilot Officer Charles Frizzell too, 'I was rather fond of Bonnie. He was in a foreign country, a long way from his home and with no close friends – a French-Canadian in an RAF squadron. I admired his courage to be a loner, and also his ability, in spite of a somewhat rough and rustic exterior, to converse fluently in French. I always had the impression that he thought his days were numbered.'[47]

Bonnie had left a note in his kitbag asking that no personal letter of condolence be sent to his mother. Indeed, he was his mother's only child.

By 10.40am that morning, Sergeant Pilot Reg Nutter had also been hit in combat and was slightly wounded. In the same raid Pilot Officer Kenneth Gundry, who had been in the squadron for just ten days, had his port tail shot off and his starboard aileron split in two; luckily he landed safely. In a letter to his parents Kenneth Gundry recorded:

> 'We separated as a flight and found ourselves sitting under about eighty Me 110 fighters milling

[47]Letter to Geoff Rayner, July 28 1981

> around in a huge circle. Above them were about fifty or more Me 109s. The next thing I knew was a ruddy great earthquake in my aircraft and my control column was almost solid. On my left another Hurricane was floating about over a complete network of smoke trails left by cannon shells and incendiary.'[48]

It was no wonder that so many 257 planes had been lost in the aerial chaos and against such large enemy numbers. There was one consolation for Gundry. 'One poor Ju 88 was spotted going back from a raid and about seven of us whooped for joy and dived on him from all directions. He finally went down in a complete inferno of red-hot metal and we could see the column of smoke rising from where it crashed.'

That day Terry Hunt grew worried about her husband as she waited as usual at the gate, so she telephoned RAF Martlesham Heath, hoping that Myers would answer. *'Perhaps if he had known, Geoff would have come to the phone as I always imagined someone kindly and discreet would do. As it was, when I rang at midday, it was an airman who said: "E's one of the one's o've come down."*

By degrees, I discovered that David was in hospital in a place that sounded like the Highlands of Scotland.'

An hour and a half later on the dot, Terry rang back as requested. *'This time they sent Charles Frizzell to the telephone. He had been at the party. He was someone I knew. He told me that David had been shot down by parachute and burned... I said to Charles; "He's not*

[48]Letter to his parents August 1940: Imperial War Museum

going to die or anything?" Charles said: "Nothing like that."'

David Hunt had parachuted down and crash-landed at Brook Farm, Margaretting, in Essex.

On hearing the news about her husband, Terry immediately set off for the hospital at Billericay, with her mother accompanying her for support.

'David was lying on the bed. The newness of his accident was the sensation in the room. He himself was something brand new and very real. I saw him just for a moment, his face and arms purple with fresh dye and swollen. I thought he has no eyes; and I thought they had not told me that but had left me to find out quietly for myself; and, curiously, how wise they were. Behind all this was David. I saw then, as I cannot see now, how we should manage his blindness.'

Terry kissed her husband and recalled how red her lips were against the purple. David explained how the hood of his Hurricane jammed and trapped him but how, after a long time, he had thought about his wife and forced the hood open. *'A nurse brought the wings and buttons and the buckle off his tunic… there was a baby crying all the time. The sunlight was white and harsh outside the window. The baby cried and cried. After a time, I got up and closed the window, and made the room my home.'*

In just ten minutes that morning, 257 Squadron had lost one pilot who had been killed; another had been badly burned and a third had been wounded.

The strain on Myers, of supporting his squadron as they were being decimated, was severe. The greater the carnage in 257 the more he worried about his family in France. It was as if the world was out of control – and the twin anxieties about the tragedies in his unit, and his family's dangerous isolation, fed off each other.

In France, Margot Myers, seeing with her own eyes the increased presence of German troops, decided to head south across the demarcation line while she still could. Rumours were intensifying of a final battle not far away on the River Loire. Her plan was to escape to Spain. Her children and some other family members, including her grandmother, piled into two cars – seven of them in one little Renault – leaving only her mother and infirm relatives behind. On the road south to Thiers there were columns of troops everywhere. It was chaos.

In Thiers, the Myers family slept in their cars. The roads were jammed with vehicles and in the town square scores of people were sleeping on the ground. In the nearby village of Ste Marguerite, an elderly woman saw the two young Myers children and their great-grandmother asleep in the car and offered them a makeshift bed, much to the relief of their mother. The Germans appeared to have taken over and the town was thick with refugees. Margot was worried about how she would find enough petrol to travel further, and there were many rumours of bridges being smashed by German bombs.

At Thiers Town Hall she was, like everyone else, issued with the general advice to go home. She was offered enough petrol to do so. Margot talked it through with the rest of the family and they decided that without sufficient petrol there was no option but to return to Beaurepaire. On the journey back they almost crashed into a van full of German soldiers.

Back at home, Margot was both relieved and scared. She was pleased to see her mother again and to feel the security of a solid home around the family, but Lucenay-lès-Aix was now full of Germans. They had started impounding houses and began marching through the village carrying swastikas. How soon before they knew about a half-British family living nearby?

Margot had been only nineteen, still naïve, when she married. Now she realised she had to learn how to survive, and fast. Rumours and propaganda swirled around and there was a noticeable increase in anti-British feeling. Margot and her mother were both cautious about Pétain and any rumours of an armistice with the Germans.

Margot lit a big fire and burned photographs and anything that might reveal the British or Jewish side of the family. Other precious photographs and documents were buried by a family member, 'I never found them again. Neither did he ... did he destroy them in a moment of fear? Also, the hunting rifles that we had buried in the garden and could never find again? Fear makes one do such strange things.'[49]

It was a relief that the farmer who worked the land attached to the house had disappeared to fight. Margot and her mother worked the land and animals even harder. At least she would be able to feed her children, she thought, and the less she needed to buy food in the local village, now swarming with Nazis, the better. His children in France were also constantly in Geoff's mind.

Oh my luvvies, if only I could see you for a moment and be reassured! Perhaps I would see Robert, still playing with his little wheelbarrow under the oak tree or chopping wood in the farmyard. Does Anne still trip

[49]Memoirs of Margot Myers translated by her daughter, Anne

around with Grandma and pay daily calls on the rabbits? Is the harvest brought in and have you been left enough?

I looked at your photo yesterday, Ducky, quite calmly, as if I would be seeing you in a fortnight's time.

Pilot Officer Charles Frizzell remembered, 'We were beginning to feel a bit crumpled. We had suffered more losses than inflicted upon the enemy. I think what upset us was what we read in the newspapers, this enormous discrepancy between what we were doing and the other squadrons.'[50]

With Bonseigneur dead, and David Hunt in hospital, 257 Squadron was down to the bare bones. Even when the unit did fly, Squadron Leader Harkness was a liability. Flight Lieutenant Hugh Beresford felt the pressure intensely and despaired of Harkness.

Beresford said, 'This afternoon, [Harkness] saw all the bombs crashing below us in the oil tanks in the estuary. But do you think it made any difference to him? No, he just went on circling at 18,000 feet. He didn't seem to hear or see anything. Of course, he's scared! I know that. And look what's happening to the squadron.'

As even his local Royal Air Forces Association in Melton Mowbray put it, 'Hugh gave the men of his squadron much needed morale at a time when his CO showed the conduct of a coward by flying away from the action. Although Hugh was privately very nervous and vomited under the daily intense suicidal stress of the Battle of Britain, when the pilots were almost always greatly outnumbered – the Luftwaffe sent 1,500 planes

[50]BBC TV ' Inside Story: Missing' September 7 1980

at its height – he most bravely went straight into the attack.'[51]

In the late afternoon of September 7, just before 5.00pm, 257 Squadron – under the overall command of Harkness – was airborne for the fourth time that day to meet a huge force of more than fifty German fighters and bombers headed for London. Beresford was leading A Flight, flying Hurricane P3049, and Lancelot Mitchell was in charge of B Flight. 257 were exhausted and very low on morale. That afternoon they met the Luftwaffe over the Thames Estuary. The air was smooth, with high cirrus cloud in a blue sky. The squadron was scrambled late and struggled to get into a position they could attack the enemy from. They were outnumbered, and out of the sun the escort of German fighters dived swiftly down to attack the Hurricanes of 257.

As the RAFA Melton Mowbray recorded, 'Beresford tried to warn the other pilots of the danger over the radio, issuing a frantic warning to the squadron about the attacking fighters, stating that he could not attack as another Hurricane was in his line of fire. Then there was silence. In his final few moments of life he had used his last breath to save others… none of the squadron saw what happened to him.'

On the ground, Ashley Reeve was one of a group of men laying a pipeline; he watched the dogfights overhead. 'We saw one plane in a sort of dive. The engine was cutting, spluttering, then it picked up for the second time, roared to life and then literally disappeared into the ground.'[52]

[51]RAFA Melton Mowbray, Leicestershire
[52]BBC TV 'Inside Story: Missing' September 7 1980

By the end of the afternoon, not only was Beresford dead but the second flight leader, Lancelot Mitchell, too. The Hurricanes of Sergeants Hulbert and Robinson were badly damaged. Geoffrey Myers wrote in his notebook of his roommate.

I slept alone last night. Mitchell has gone. I can't believe that he is missing. There were his pyjamas on the bed. His violin on the table. He played to me only two nights ago. As he played, he said, 'I don't mind the noise, do you Geoff? Sorry, a string's missing. I know I'm not much good at it, but somehow…'

Now Mitchell can't be a Flight Lieutenant. It was his burning desire. He had been expecting promotion last week. After that he was going to marry his Margery. But our squadron leader had neglected to do the necessary paperwork and Mitchell never got a fair deal.

Myers remembered, 'Pilots all disappeared in the same way. In this case it cost us lives. I don't know how many. You had to be highly organised. You had to have extremely good leadership. These men were killed through no fault of their own.'[53]

In his contemporaneous notebooks Myers recalled Lancelot Mitchell's last night:

> **The night before his death he scarcely spoke to anyone. He remained in the anteroom far into the morning, writing to his Margery, to his mother and to his sister.**
>
> **He used to talk to me far into the night. He talked about Margery. 'I don't think she will let**

[53]BBC TV ' Inside Story: Missing' September 7 1980

me down. She's the most wonderful woman in the world. Don't smile. I know I've said that before.'

There was really something about Mitchell that attracted women and they really intended to get married, I think. They had been telling everyone in the mess that the wedding was for the next month. Now Margery will wait awhile for another man.

Hugh Beresford had already been recently married to Pat, who was only nineteen. It was almost coming up to their first wedding anniversary. In his secret letters to his family, Geoff Myers observed Pat's grief.

Hugh Beresford. Another hero gone. Mrs Beresford rang up last night. She was in tears. The adjutant tries to soothe her over the telephone. He didn't quite know what he was saying, spoke about boats that might have picked Beresford up at sea. We told her not to give up hope but she knew. She asked if she could fetch his clothes. 'She sounds sweet,' the adjutant said. He was almost in tears himself. He had a double whisky after that.

Beresford was the real leader of the squadron. The strain under which he was living penetrated my system, and I could do nothing for him. It was tough.

For weeks, Myers had been trying to get Harkness moved. He felt disloyal but he knew it was the right thing to do. 257 squadron had been decimated. The effect on those who remained was transparent. Young Carl Capon was the favourite of Myers. **'He was my own personal hero. He was so pure. Even if he knew he could be shot down, this was his job and he was going to stick to it. He'd never leave anyone in the lurch.'**

He did not think he was much good and I tried to encourage him by telling him what I thought of his keenness and bravery.

Geoffrey had real concerns about Carl Capon and the impact another disastrous day in the skies would have on someone who was courageous but lacking in confidence.

Poor Capon will go crackers if we don't look out. He's just twenty and to look at him with his innocent earnest blue eyes, his open face and wide forehead under that light wavy hair, you would think he was not yet eighteen. He would follow his leader anywhere in the sky and never let them down whatever the odds against them.

Tonight, he couldn't stop writhing as he sat on the table with his hands. 'There were too many of them. They sailed down the Thames Estuary in perfect formation. And we did nothing. They just bombed us and went back.'

Carl Capon was going to buy a second-hand car from Freddie Wallis, the adjutant, and accused Wallis of planning to claim it back quickly because Capon would soon be killed.

The adjutant had intended nothing of the kind. 'Don't be silly old man,' he said. 'Silly! What's silly in that?' Capon asked. 'Just count up the squadron now and think for yourself. On August 8 we were twenty-six and now what's left of us? Nine?'

The loss of two flight leaders on one day and a missed rendezvous with other squadrons finally pushed 11 Group HQ into moving Squadron Leader Harkness to a training role at RAF Boscombe Down.

My Ducky, I had a painful day again today. What I had been working for, for weeks, happened and I knew that it would cut me up when the day came. Yesterday evening the Squadron went up and should have met another squadron over London to intercept raiders. They missed each other and the AOC [Air Officer Commanding the Group] was annoyed. He put through an inquiry. It turned out that it was no fault of our squadron. But on previous occasions there had been so many muddles in which Harkness was at fault that this must have been drawn to the attention of the AOC. The opportunity was used to relieve Harkness of his command.

Harkness came to me saying, 'They've just told me over the phone that I'm to hand over the squadron to Stanford Tuck.' I couldn't say anything. I couldn't be hypocritical enough to say I am sorry. Rotten business, because we personally got on well together and he regarded me as his friend.

In fact, it was Squadron Leader Robert Stanford Tuck who was finally responsible for the downfall of Hill Harkness. He had been posted to 257 along with his very capable colleague, Pete Brothers, to replace the two leaders, Beresford and Mitchell. Brothers recalled what happened when they flew with the squadron, alongside Harkness, to patrol a line above Maidstone at 20,000 feet. The squadron had seen a large formation of bombers with fighter escorts approaching and alerted the squadron leader. 'He [Harkness] said, "We've been told to patrol the Maidstone line and that's what we'll do until we are told otherwise." So we all pissed off and left him and got stuck in.'[54]

[54]Patrick Bishop, *Fighter Boys* (HarperCollins, 2004)

In his biography, Pete Brothers took a slightly more understanding line about Harkness. 'Too old for the game. He was probably thirty or thirty-five and he was past it from our point of view – too cautious after the heavy losses – possibly had relied on the tactical abilities of his two flight commanders.'[55]

Initially, Brothers worried that he and Tuck had made a misjudgement about Harkness, 'But then this happened a second time, then a third time and we decided that this chap just wanted to avoid combat at all costs.' Fortified by a few drinks they rang up Keith Park, who was the Commander of 11 Group and one of the most senior figures in Fighter Command. They asked that Harkness be sacked. Clearly, Park listened because Harkness was then removed and sent back to a training role at Boscombe Down. Other pilots suffering from 'lack of moral fibre' were put on more menial duties.[56]

In his biography of Pete Brothers, Nick Thomas is kinder to Harkness arguing that despite his senior years as a fighter pilot, Harkness had elected to fly operationally whenever he could. He was right that Harkness was just too old in a sky full of pilots ten or fifteen years younger than him. But the notebooks of Geoffrey Myers are unequivocal when he writes about the shortcomings of Harkness – and these flaws were confirmed by others in 257.

After telling me he had been posted, Harkness gave me an appealing look, as if to say, 'Well, Geoff, it was not my fault.' My eyes did not reply. He was cut up for about half an hour. Then he suggested going out to the cinema together. It really seemed as if the loss of his

[55]Nick Thomas, *Hurricane Squadron Ace* (Pen and Sword, 2014)
[56]Larry Forrester, *Fly for Your Life* (Frederick Muller, 1956)

command had already ceased to worry him. Curious man, with round shifting eyes and changing pupils like those of a bird. Curiously shaped head too – an egg with a bump behind. His vanity saved him. He always argued and he always assumed that everybody else was wrong.

When Gundry heard that Harkness was leaving the squadron his eyes lighted up and he said, 'I suppose I shouldn't say "Whoopee" but that's how I feel.'

That's how we all felt. But Beresford, who could have pulled the squadron round by himself alone, had gone a week too early. And Mitchell had gone without being made an Acting Flight Lieutenant.

In Billericay Hospital, Terry Hunt waited anxiously to know if her husband would live, let alone see again. The doctor told her that he would not know until the next day if David Hunt would live or die.

'Geoff rang up, a sane and friendly voice, and asked for details so that he could make his report. I went like an echo to and fro along the corridor, from the telephone to the bed and back again. Dry facts were what we gave: the time, the place and his position in the formation; though I remember that Geoff rang again to ask what colour the flashes from the cannon had been, and that would be picturesque.'

They also discussed her husband's lucky scarf and Myers offered to help. '*Would Geoff find David's Lucky Scarf for him? He had never flown without it, without some small thing happening; and a fortnight ago he had left it behind in a plane. Geoff would do his best.*'

The next day Terry Hunt heard the news she had been waiting for, '*The doctor came to me in the corridor, and told me that he had been out of danger and was going under his own steam after all. He asked how long we had been married, and I told him nine weeks. He looked amused but they still did not know about his eyes. Until he opened them, they could not know if he would see.'*

The full picture of what happened to David Hunt finally emerged and he described what happened on that fateful September 3. '*A dazzling array of multicoloured light appeared on the starboard side of the cockpit, accompanied by explosive concussions. Immediately, flame came through the instrument panel, filling the cockpit and burning my hands, legs and face. The reserve fuel tank had exploded and I had neither gloves nor goggles, which I had pushed over my forehead in order to get a better view. I then tried to open the hood but found it had jammed. Using both hands on one side, I managed to pull the hood open, undid my Sutton harness, grabbed my helmet off and plunged out of the starboard side of the plane. I started to survey the damage. My hands were all bloody, like I was feeling and they were covered with projecting tissue; that was the skin; and all that was left of my sleeve was a charred ribbon of rank.*'

David Hunt was worried about being shot at on the way down but nothing happened. He was struck by the stillness and peace, as he floated down towards the ground. '*All I could hear now was the fluttering of the canopy, which reminded me of a yacht, and the fading drone and crackle of the battle going on above. There was a scrape, a swing and then a light bump. I had landed. I lay as I was for a time, then sat up, and leant my arm downwards so that the ridiculous ribbon fell off my wrist, attached by a single thread.*'

Chapter Seven

Robert Stanford Tuck was probably the most famous pilot to emerge from the Battle of Britain. By the time he arrived at the dispirited 257 Squadron, he was already a legend. Tall, thin-faced with slicked back hair and a moustache, he looked like a man about town playing roulette on the French Riviera, but there was no mistaking his courage and skill in the air. Geoffrey Myers was delighted to see the departure of Squadron Leader Harkness, but he was also cautious about Tuck's reputation.

Some weeks ago, I tried to write to you about Stanford Tuck. I could not put the words down, so I tried to write in code. I had something very secret that I wanted to say, but the code would not work and I fell asleep while struggling with it. Now I will write in clear.

When he took over command of our squadron, he was regarded as a hero. He soon told me of all the aircraft he had shot down. Something like eighteen. Most of his claims seemed a bit hazy to me, but that did not matter. The very sight of him seemed to give confidence to the boys.

He thought that Tuck could inspire the demoralised pilots of 257. In *Fly for Your Life*, his biography of Tuck, Larry Forrester describes Pilot Officer Geoffrey Myers as 'small, plump and fortyish – a foreign correspondent for a big national daily before the war. He was a placid, soft-voiced and gentle-eyed Jewish intellectual.'

Geoff Myers clearly looked older than his years as he was then only thirty-four, still some years away from being 'fortyish'. Forrester described the first meeting between Squadron Leader Stanford Tuck and the men at 257 who were now under his command. 'They were a sorry-looking lot. Scruffy, listless and leaderless, they were quarrelling among themselves over trivialities, drinking hard but entirely without zest. Over the last few weeks they had taken a severe mauling – this was probably the only squadron in Fighter Command to lose more aircraft than they'd shot down. For all their failures and frustrations they blamed "organised chaos up top." They really believed they were being betrayed by their leaders.'

That was not an unreasonable view held by the pilots. After all, they had been trained on Spitfires and then mysteriously retrained on Hurricanes. Then their 'leaders' had been surgically removed; against his will, the superb boss who was effectively shaping them into a coherent fighting unit had been replaced with a weak and incompetent squadron leader transferred from a training unit.

The other new arrival as flight leader, Peter Brothers, from Lancashire, was a crucial support to Tuck as they tried to knock 257 into shape. When he was still at school in Manchester, Brothers had learned to fly, aged just sixteen. Brothers was more understanding than Tuck of the pressures on the young pilots of 257. 'Morale in the squadron was way down the bottom, naturally. They were a bunch of young chaps, only two of them with pre-war experience. The others were chaps with minimum training. Naturally they were thinking, if these two experienced chaps [Beresford and Mitchell] can be shot down, what sort of chance have we got?'[57]

Tuck was lucky to have Brothers at his right hand. 'Pete Brothers turned out to be a corker. He was highly intelligent and devoted to his job – an excellent flight commander.'[58]

Tuck would have just a few days to sort out the chaos and knock 257 into good enough shape to fight the Luftwaffe again. As Forrester wrote, 'To them [257] he seemed a lean, mean and vainglorious person. He had a dry, arrogant face and he walked with his head held high, like a blind man. The immaculate uniform, the glossy hair and the 'Cesar Romero' moustache kindled their instinctive scorn for all forms of bull-shine. It was true that, outwardly, he often seemed a noisy show-off and a bit of a fop, too. Lately, he had taken to using a long, slim cigarette holder and his mannerisms were very haughty indeed!'

On arrival, Tuck and the pilots studiously ignored each other. Myers was puzzled as he waited while Tuck downed pint after pint. 'Geoff stared at the mug in his hand. He couldn't think what it was doing there. He disliked beer – never accepted a pintful – at a push he could make half a pint, forced upon him, last all night. Geoff wondered whether to perform the introductions, but decided to wait until Tuck gave him a clear hint. Geoff didn't notice the first of them [the pilots] drift over. He only knew that suddenly they were shaking hands with Tuck, looking a bit sheepish, and telling him

[57]Patrick Bishop, *Fighter Boys* (HarperCollins, 2004)
[58]Larry Forrester, *Fly for Your Life* (Frederick Muller, 1956)

their names, and he was buying them drinks. And then, in no time at all, he had one or two of them talking – cautiously at first, and then, with amazing candour.'

Myers was impressed with the man-management skills of Tuck, who gradually dominated the conversations with the bedraggled group of pilots, his questions growing more forensic by the minute. Myers could see that he was winning some of the men round. 'Most of the pilots remained silent, suspicious and some openly hostile. But Myers was amazed, and deeply stirred, to see their faces losing their blank, wrenched expressions, the eyes coming alive for the first time in weeks.'

For the first time since Squadron Leader David Bayne had been unceremoniously shunted out of the unit at the beginning of the Battle of Britain, Myers felt some grounds for optimism. Here was a man, for all his surface glamour, who he knew deep down to be a fine pilot. But Tuck also seemed to have the ability to win over the disaffected and the angry.

Larry Forrester had clearly interviewed Myers at length for his biography of Stanford Tuck. 'Myers had knocked round the world enough to know that no man, no matter how gifted or successful, was without human failings, and he tried to decide what Tuck's faults might be. He guessed – and he wasn't far wrong – that intolerance of others' weaknesses might be one, snap judgement another. Myers the writer, the student of human character who vaguely sensed this, had an opportunity to confirm some of his theories later that night.'

Tuck and Myers had dinner and then went to the orderly room together. Tuck, all the jollity of the beer-drinking gone, was very direct. 'Right, let's have it.

I know the squadron's record – what a miserable shower of bloody deadbeats! Not worth a bag of nuts as far as I can see. Now, you're going to tell me which of them are worth salvaging, and which should be given the boot.'

Myers, loath to accept the responsibility, raised his hands, shoulders and eyebrows in an ancient Hebraic gesture, but before he could protest, Tuck smashed his fist down on the trestle table between them and positively snarled, 'Look, if you're going to stay on here yourself, you'd better get on my side right this minute. I want the personal record of every pilot. I'll see their files later – first I want your opinions, the straight gen, and no bloody nonsense.'

Myers slowly began to tell Tuck what he needed to hear, commending Pete Brothers, Jimmy Cochrane, and Jock Girdwood, among others. As Tuck's biography put it, 'Myers knew all right. He had a deep affection for every one of these young men and he understood their terrible disillusionment and bitterness. He had watched their spirits ebb and their cynicism grow, and he had lain awake for many a night because there was nothing he could do to help them.'

Over the next few days, Myers saw a different side of Bob Stanford Tuck. He studied the personal files of every pilot with great care and Myers could see that, for all his flamboyance, he was a meticulous pilot, forever checking and rechecking the working order of his Hurricane and its guns. Tuck immediately set about restoring confidence and discipline in the embattled squadron at Martlesham Heath. He even grew to like the Hurricane which he had initially described, compared to the sleek Spitfire, 'like flying a brick – a great lumbering farmyard stallion compared with a dainty and gentle thoroughbred.'[59] Indeed, he admired the gun platform, and the visibility for the pilot was better. The Hurricane was heavier to handle but easier to land, and it was just as well powered as any other fighter in the world.

Several new pilots arrived around the same time as Tuck. They replaced the young men who had been killed or injured. Among them were Pilot Officer Percy Mortimer from Wales, Pilot Officer Jan Pfeiffer – a Pole, and Flying Officer Alan Hedges. They were later joined by John Martin from New Zealand and the Scot, Jack Kay. Between them these new flyers had little or no experience of aerial warfare. 257 was, as before, a mixed bag of personalities and nationalities for Tuck and Brothers to lick into shape.

For three days, according to Forrester, Tuck and Brothers tutored the squadron intensively. The new boss immediately abandoned the inflexible tactics favoured by Hill Harkness, introducing flying in pairs and loosening the formations. He taught the unit how to exploit the weaknesses of the Luftwaffe in the air and to not waste bullets by firing from too long a range. Tuck carefully explained all the reasons for the changes. The only break in the drill was to refuel or a quick lunch from a hot box. In the evenings there was no heading for the pub. Tuck gave lectures in the briefing room, explaining the blind spots of German bombers. Models were built by the fitters so he could explain the best angles of attack. The pilots were given intelligence reports that analysed other, more successful, squadrons and learned about engine revs and throttle positions.

[59]Larry Forrester *Fly for Your Life* Frederick Muller 1956

Although the operational records do not fully corroborate the intense training, Sergeant Reg Nutter could immediately see the improvement. 'I found him to be a very charismatic leader and this, combined with his exceptional combat record, gave one a great deal of confidence in him. His style of leadership contrasted greatly with that of his predecessor, Squadron Leader Harkness. Tuck would make suggestions to the ground controller as to how we might be better placed to intercept, but Harkness would follow instructions slavishly. There was no doubt that before Tuck's arrival the squadron's morale was at a low ebb. Under his leadership there was a tremendous improvement. In many ways he was an individualist but he would nevertheless go out of his way to give sound advice to other pilots.'[60]

Myers himself later reflected, 'Tuck wanted to know everything about the squadron. It made me feel he was the right man for the job.'[61]

Larry Forrester noted in his book, 'Myers was astounded by the metamorphosis. After deep thought he attributed it to the simple fact that Tuck so obviously knew his trade and fortunately had the ability to explain things lucidly.'

By the third day of Tuck's leadership the improvement was significant. Even the most sceptical of the pilots in 257 were won over by Tuck's sheer professionalism. Nearly all of them felt more confident in the air. Tuck told Group HQ that he was progressing well and that his squadron would be ready for combat earlier than

[60]Battle of Britain Monument
[61]Interview with Author, 1981

expected, in three or four days, but he was informed that Fighter Command could not wait that long. Pilots and planes were at a dangerously low level and every single aircraft and pilot would be needed for the climax of the Battle. Group HQ knew that the next few days would be the most critical in the Battle of Britain and no squadron, even one as embattled as 257, could be spared.

As luck would have it, Tuck was at a conference in Debden and missed the big morning scramble on Battle of Britain Day, Sunday September 15 1940. It was a bright, windless day and the Luftwaffe sent 1,120 aircraft, a mix of bombers and escort fighters, to hammer southern England.

The squadron went up under the command of the new Flight Lieutenant, Pete Brothers, whom everyone liked as soon as they met him. His movements were so quick you could never be quite sure if he was facing you or turning his back. He was like that in the air too.

At midday, Brothers and eight other pilots were airborne. Pilot Officer Jimmy Cochrane was one of the first to land after the Blitz. Cochrane was angry about being shot at by the ack-ack guns of British defences.

But Jesus! Our ack-ack fire's a bugger! I saw a direct hit on one poor devil in a Hurricane which burst into flames and broke into bits in the air. The poor chap hadn't time to bail out, I guess. The crazy devils! Not a single Jerry plane anywhere near us. The ack-ack was after us all right. Thought we were Jerries.

Sergeant Robinson also came down cursing the anti-aircraft guns. 'Bloody disgraceful firing into the middle of us, with nothing else around.'

As Myers recorded again in his notebook, not all of the pilots had yet been transformed by Tuck's magic.

One Sergeant Pilot Squire, who had never flown in combat before, returned from that first sortie looking deeply anxious.

'I didn't quite know what happened,' he said, 'I suppose it's because I haven't got into the way of things yet. I expect I'll get my nerve next time.' I did not press him. It was his first encounter with the enemy and obviously something had gone wrong.

'Come and sit down, old man,' I said. 'Don't worry, lots of chaps get queer turns at the beginning.' When he felt a bit reassured, he said, 'I passed clean out at 14,000 feet. No, it wasn't a blackout or anything. The sight of all those bombers just made me feel queer and I fainted. It's a poor show and I find it difficult to explain.' I quickly put in my word, 'You needn't worry about that sort of thing, old chap. The first time the boys went up in a blitz, they all felt a bit queer.'

It had been a hot, windless day. Just as the squadron were having lunch the telephone bell rang and the operations clerk in the neighbouring tent yelled out, 'Scramble!'

They grabbed their yellow life jackets – their Mae West's as they were called – from their beds and dashed out to their aeroplanes which had all been re-serviced. The operations clerk yelled out the full order, 'Scramble angels fifteen over Duxford.'

Just as they were about to depart, Tuck arrived back from Debden. He immediately grabbed a Mae West and took Squire's plane since the young pilot, as Tuck's biographer kindly put it, was not feeling too well.

A massive attack was being launched on London, the strongest mounted in daylight during the Battle of Britain so far. There were scores of Luftwaffe bombers escorted by fighter squadrons of Messerschmitts. The total was around 250 enemy aircraft, all headed for London, and with a huge bombload.

Not all the Hurricanes from 257 were airborne.

One plane failed to take off. It was Frizzell's. I went to see what was the matter. 'That's the second time today that my plane's refused to start up,' he said. 'I seem to miss all the big shows. It is a damned shame!' Frizzell spoke without much conviction. I knew he was glad to be out of it. He guessed what I was thinking. 'It's not that I particularly enjoy a blitz,' he said, 'but I don't like letting the other boys down. Nobody enjoys the blitzes, I'm quite sure, and I don't mind telling you I'm shit scared of them, and that all the others are too. Some of them pretend they're not but if you talk it over intimately, you'll find they're all shit scared like me.'

He was a boy of nineteen who had been thrown headlong into battle with his ideas in complete turmoil. He was not born to be a fighter pilot and was acutely conscious of this.

In fact, Frizzell was wrong about himself. He went through the war as a successful pilot and finished up commanding a squadron.

The small band of Hurricanes was significantly outnumbered by the Luftwaffe. The enemy reached the south-eastern edge of London untroubled. 257 knew they could make an interception but they were beneath the enemy planes when they arrived and the Germans had the advantage of height. Tuck and his pilots had no choice but to attack. They ignored the German fighters and headed for the bombers, the Heinkels and Junkers ahead. As Tuck tried to shoot down a bomber, an Me

109 headed straight for him. For a second, Tuck thought that he would die on this course but he managed to climb away in a steep turn, swiftly followed by Pilot Officer Carl Capon.

Ahead they saw a group of Me 110 fighter-bombers making a turn. Tuck swiftly lined one up and fired. The 110 burst into flames. While Carl Capon followed a Heinkel as it headed down and away, Tuck waited for a second German fighter to appear. The Luftwaffe fought in pairs and he knew that a second plane would be in attendance. Tuck was right. As the enemy plane crossed in front of Tuck's Hurricane he fired again and the German aircraft spun swiftly downwards, bellowing smoke.

As the pilots from 257 looked around the blue sky it was strangely empty and eerily quiet. All Tuck could see was a single parachute drifting slowly downwards to the south.

Back at base, Myers waited anxiously for the pilots to return. Any sense of joy was muted when they arrived home because Stanford Tuck, Pete Brothers and Carl Capon were missing. Surely, thought Myers, we can't have lost our leaders again, so soon after their predecessors, Hugh Beresford and Lancelot Mitchell, had been shot down?

West was the first to land from the second blitz. He couldn't speak and had to rush off. He had been sick all over his uniform just as the squadron was entering into the enemy formation. He had to return quickly. West was no coward. He was a typical brave young lad. But he was new to air fighting and did not know that his stomach would play tricks on him with a half digested meal when he faced the enemy at 15,000 feet.

While Myers waited for the missing men, Jimmy Cochrane landed.

'Anything doing?' I asked him. His hands were still trembling with the excitement of the battle. He had not even had time to take off his helmet. His eyes were still wild, as he began to speak.

Jimmy was sure he had shot down a German plane but, as other fighters were close by, he wasn't sure if he could claim a 'kill'.

Cochrane had been smart again. He and two other members of his section had swooped down on a Heinkel 111 and had emptied all their ammunition into it. His eyes, like two daggers, seemed to pierce the Heinkel again as he told me how it went down.

The operational records had the German aircraft as a Dornier 17 rather than a Heinkel but the end result was the same. The 257 pilots, led by Jimmy Cochrane, saw two crew members bail out and then the pilot brought the aircraft down safely in the thick mud.

'Oh! It was a luscious sight! We circled round the two fellows as they sailed down in their parachutes. I bet they went through a few uncomfortable moments when we flew round them. They must have been wondering whether we'd machine-gun them as they had been doing to our boys, the bastards!

As Jimmy Cochrane put it in his combat report, 'After six or seven bursts the E/A [enemy aircraft] turned over and went down in a spin, one parachutist leaving the smoking Do17. Just above the clouds the machine blew into bits.'[62]

The euphoria continued.

[62]National Archives, Kew

The phone rang in the tent. The controller ordered the ambulance and the fire squad to go out on the field. Gundry had been shot up and was not sure if he could land. His Hurricane circled twice round the aerodrome, dipped slightly, bounced a bit and settled down in a gentle run across the field. When Gundry put his head out of the cockpit he had a twinkle in his eye. He noticed my amazement. The whole of his port tailplane had been shot away and tatters of canvas were hanging from his main plane. Petrol was streaming out of his tanks.

Miraculously, Gundry had made it home and, more than that, he had additional success to tell:

> 'I got the bugger who did it. At least, I can't claim him as 'destroyed', but I damaged him all right, because I saw the fabric hanging from his tailplane, much like mine. I shouldn't think he got back, poor devil. There must have been thirty or forty of them when we intercepted them south-east of London. I doubt if many of them got back again. There seemed to be hundreds of Hurricanes and Spitfires in the air. It was a lovely sight. We really seem to have got it taped now. Before, when we went up, we seemed to be alone, but now it's quite different.'

But celebration of success was stilled. Tuck, Brothers and Capon were all still missing.

The bag was the best the squadron had had in one day. Eight 'destroyed' or 'probably destroyed' as we classified them. Three damaged. But nobody felt in the mood for rejoicing about that. No Tuck, no Brothers

and still no word about Capon. I was getting more and more fidgety. I tried not to show the boys my concern.

The minutes were slipping by. Soon they would be out of petrol. By now, all the other pilots who had returned were lying on their beds lined up in two rows. The BBC announcer was already talking about the Thames Estuary Blitz. They listened to him with complete indifference, knowing that the details would be received only hours later. We were still all waiting for news of Brothers and Capon.

Myers waited at the dispersal point with Jimmy Cochrane, who always called it 'desperation point'.

I could still not believe that we were in for another black day but I was haunted by what happened at the last blitz when neither of the flight commanders came back.

The rest of the squadron were put on a quarter of an hour availability and were fetched up to the mess for tea. Then, the anxious Geoffrey Myers had a telephone call to tell him that Tuck had refuelled at another airfield and was safely on his way back.

Faces brightened up at that, although everyone had felt pretty sure he would turn up.

When Tuck finally landed, Myers told him that 257 had been credited with shooting down several enemy aircraft and, although two senior pilots were missing they had, as yet, suffered no confirmed losses themselves. The enthusiastic groundcrew stencilled two more swastikas on Tuck's Hurricane, making a total of sixteen.

Tuck came back and wrote out a personal combat report for two enemy aircraft destroyed and one probable.

No sooner had the pilots arrived in the mess than word came through that Brothers was about to land in his own plane. Two of us rushed down to the dispersal point.

Pete Brothers had suffered damage to his aileron controls but RAF Biggin Hill, where he landed, had failed to inform 257 that Brothers was safe. He had also shot down a Dornier 215. Despite returning late, the only thought of Pete Brothers was to get back into the air.

Brothers immediately started to superintend the refuelling and rearming of another Hurricane placed at his disposal. He darted around from one side to another to see that everything was in order. Today was his ninth bag and the first time he had been hit. Before going up to the mess he darted into my tent and looked at the preliminary report of the battle. When he saw 'Flt Lt Peter Brothers D.F.C, missing', his face became flushed but he said nothing. 'We've got to do that after a few hours,' I told him, 'so that there can be a check-up at Air Ministry. We all felt sure you would turn up.'

Myers was particularly fond of young Carl Capon, his 'personal hero', adding that 'he was like a schoolboy, uncertain of himself, but he was going to do everything that he could in his own way. Even if he knew he could be shot down this was his job, and he was going to stick to it. He was pure.'[63]

So Myers could not relax – even though both Tuck and Brothers were back in one piece – until Carl Capon also joined them safely at the aerodrome.

We went back to the mess for tea. Tuck was actually saying that it didn't look too good for Capon when there was a phone call from dispersal to say that he was just about to land.

[63]Interview with Author

Myers and others rushed down to fetch Capon, who reported, **'I got shot up and went right through the London balloon barrage. Don't know how I missed one of them. They fixed my plane up at Croydon. I expect the telephone must have been bombed, or something, as they were dropping their eggs around there before I landed.' There was terrific excitement in the mess. Everybody back without a scratch! The squadron's luck had turned.**

Fighter Command had successfully resisted the largest raid ever mounted by the Luftwaffe and 257 Squadron, 'the deadbeats' – as Tuck had called them – had played their full part. Tuck himself later concluded that 'September 15 was one of the most important days of my life. It was the day that 257 became a squadron, and after that they never looked back.'

Myers recalled, 'It was one of the most extraordinary things. Marvellous. At these terrific odds we were winning – saving Britain against invasion.'

Myers meticulously recorded the successes.

I had expected a record, but the figure fairly took my breath away.

Chapter Eight

September 15 was a great day for the RAF, as well as for 257 Squadron, and the pilots all went out to celebrate. Forrester's biography records that, 'Tuck was the pivot of the party, pacemaker in the drinking and the loudest – if not the most tuneful – of the songsters.'

We started the evening in the White Horse with drinks all round in the public bar. Brothers kept things going by telling anecdotes in rapid succession. We then went to the Nine Nines Club of the local sports airfield which had opened its doors to the RAF. Stanford Tuck started calling the barmaid Mamouchka. 'Don't you think she looks like Mamouchka, Geoff?' he asked, 'I think it fits her very well. Come along boys. Another round.' Brothers had got behind the bar and was making the perfect imitation of a barman going down the steps into the cellar. Uproarious laughter. Mustard, as we called Capon, had got hold of a broom and was perfectly happy dusting the bar and all its inmates.

A pilot from another squadron was already at the Nine Nines Club and joined the rumbustious celebrations of 257. He was accompanied by his wife, Maggie.

Poor Maggie seemed to be waging a perpetual fight for equality with him. He was refined and she was not. He married her almost by mistake after spending an evening drinking with her. After their marriage he let

no opportunity go by to show her that he resented her presence. And yet he continued to go around with her.

Jimmy Cochrane and Charles Frizzell eventually joined the rest of the squadron just before midnight, and the drinking and hilarity went on beyond.

On the way back to the aerodrome Frizzell, in whose car I was riding, drove slap into a concrete defence block on the road. Brothers, with the rest of the squadron in his sports Bentley or on horseback on the mudguards, crashed into our rear. I got out as best I could – or at least I thought I did – with blood streaming from my forehead. I thought I tried to help Jimmy Cochrane out of the tangled mess. I was put on the grass bordering the road. Gundry was placed beside me. 'I can't remember a thing,' he said. 'Where are we? What happened? Why are we sitting here?' I struggled to remember and repeated everything that came into my head.

Other reports identified Bob Stanford Tuck as the driver of the car that smashed into the vehicle that Myers was riding in. The website for the Battle of Britain Monument recorded, 'On 15 September, Charles Frizzell was injured in an accident at Martlesham Heath when Squadron Leader RRS Tuck drove into the back of his car.' Tuck's biography made no mention of the crash. No doubt, putting two precious pilots out of action after a night of drinking was not expected of a squadron leader. Nonetheless, whoever was driving, the end result was the same.

We ended up in the local hospital. The nurses were rather disappointed to find that we had been injured in a car accident and not in the air, but this made no difference to their kind treatment. We were extraordinarily lucky.

Jimmy Cochrane and Charles Frizzell are still in bed. They will probably remain there for some months. I am up and only have two or three scars to show for the accident.

Myers was consumed by relief that the accident had not been worse but was also angry that valuable pilots had been injured on a drunken car journey and not from fighting the Luftwaffe. He wrote to his wife:

> **What would you have said, Ducky, if years later you would have learnt that I had been killed in a car crash after a night out at two bars? I know what a good many wives would have said but I believe you would have put two and two together. You would probably have guessed that I made an effort to be sociable with the boys and not to damp the enthusiasm of that night. You would probably imagine me getting behind the bar and pouring whiskies. Yes, Ducky, I think I was doing my job.**

While Myers was convalescing, 257 Squadron were still in frequent action under its fresh leadership. The worst disaster was when Sergeant Donald Aslin, flying P3643, was shot down over Detling in Kent. He bailed out but suffered serious burns and shock and was eventually moved to the legendary McIndoe Burns Unit at East Grinstead where he became part of the exclusive Guinea Pig Club. Aslin had only joined 257 Squadron the previous day.

In Billericay Hospital Terry Hunt, still nursing her badly burned husband, David, reflected. *'Already those first September days were something vivid with distance;*

the planes so clear and bright in a sky full of haze, and the sirens with a special quality to them: a clarity and purpose that familiarity had obscured; and there was so much sun, and the air itself vibrating with excitement; and David out of it all in his bed.'

For the next few weeks, Myers only heard of what was happening back in his squadron second-hand. He wrote to his family from the convalescent home where he had been transferred after a bomb had exploded close to the hospital where he'd originally been taken.

I am surrounded by willows and elms and pine trees. I've sketched this place for you, Ducky, and thought I would make another drawing for you tomorrow. But I won't after all because I have succeeded in leaving the place. I didn't want to get stuck here for weeks when I felt all right. I want to get back to work as soon as I can.

The stupidity of the accident and his good fortune in surviving continued to play on his mind. Reflections on both mortality and faith swirled around him.

My love, I didn't realise what a lucky escape I had in that road accident nearly a fortnight ago. Tuck told me in the mess last night that none of us moved after the car had crashed into the defence block. He and Pete [Brothers] pulled Cochrane and me out of the car. I thought I had jumped out myself. 'You were certainly not in a state to jump out, Geoff,' he told me, 'You were completely dazed and stood there with Gundry like reeling shadows until we put you on the roadside where you effectively held your cuts together with a handkerchief until they were bound up. It is an extraordinary thing that you were not all killed.'

I have been thinking a good deal about this accident, and also about my prayers. I have been asking myself,

'Why am I alive? How is it that I have been so lucky with the bombing?' Certainly I want to remain alive because of seeing you all again, and being useful to you when the war is over makes me want to live on. But that is no explanation. With an entirely personal God it is hard to fathom personal occurrences. One calls them 'luck' or 'providence'. This appears to be one of the reasons for the great appeal of Christianity. It seems to have added to Judaism a bridge over which one can step to God.

Of course, convalescence also gave Myers more time to think about his trapped family.

I looked at your photo yesterday, Ducky, quite calmly as if I was seeing you in a fortnight's time. I showed it to Jimmy and Charlie, and they also saw Robert and Anne. I remained calm all the time. They didn't know what I was going through. Good. I am improving. I can look at your photo and be a man.

We had seven wonderful years, my Love. We may have no more on earth. You may never see my letters. And yet we are bound up in each other in the scheme of things eternal.

Myers was determined to get back to work and support 257 Squadron. When he heard that the doctor would be visiting he took a four-mile walk on his newly unstitched foot, just to prove to the medic that he was fully fit.

The doctor, like a sensible man, concluded that I was well enough to leave [the convalescence home] and he told me if I wanted to go I could come back with him to the hospital in the ambulance.

The doctor immediately signed Geoffrey off for a few days' leave before he rejoined the squadron at Martlesham Heath. For his brief time off, Geoff stayed at a cottage near Chinnor in Oxfordshire, which belonged to a friend of his mother's.

October 1 1940

I walked up the hill. It is a little cottage in a big garden, cut into the brow of a hill, with a dozen trees clustering around it. Plenty of room for a big vegetable garden. Fields all around. A small paradise. The sort of cottage for which I would have looked for years to get for our little family.

When I am with the squadron doing my work I don't have so much time to think, but, when I'm on leave, it's different. I am most of the time with you, and have difficulty remaining with the others and not showing that I am far away. Then I start wondering.

I am sure you are strong, Ducky, and brave. I have great confidence in you. I adore you. My feelings are constantly overflowing like water rippling over a deep pool at the waterfall.

Inevitably, Myers compared the Oxfordshire farm to Beaurepaire, Margot's family house in occupied France.

Tonight I went down the hill to the farm. It had the atmosphere and smell of Beaurepaire. Even the old pump was at the sink. It made me think of the electric pump we hoped to install at Beaurepaire. What happened to the trench I was digging? Robert was expecting his Daddy to come back and finish it. He was expecting his Daddy to keep the invader away from Beaurepaire. What does he think now? I try to peer into the future and I wonder how an end can come to this disaster which has overwhelmed us all.

Myers was also tormented by the question of whether he had been wrong to leave his family in Beaurepaire.

The house had been a place of safety before and he thought that Margot's family needed their daughter with them.

I dared not believe what I feared was coming last May. When there was still time for me to call you and ask you to come. I could have said, 'Come,' but I would have asked you to leave your family, who had given you and the children a safe home, just at the moment when disaster was facing them. I could not have left them myself at that time, and I did not think that you would, so I struggled inwardly and knew you would not be coming.

Since then I have tormented myself hundreds of times, feeling that I did the wrong thing. I constantly ask myself that old, old question. Would it have been better for all if you and the children had left? Did I act rightly? What a calamity for you, my Beloved! Be strong in your thoughts. I am with you, and you are not alone. And if, by chance, I may stop writing to you and the ink runs dry before its term, I shall still be with you. A little particle of God will keep me burning within you and give you courage.

Goodnight my Love, Goodnight Robert, Goodnight Anne.

In central France, Margot and her children were surviving but she was acutely aware that one day they would be discovered. 'I was in a state of total uncertainty. What to do? Attempt to flee before the controls became stricter? But go where?'[64] Now there was no petrol. Even a bicycle was a precious possession but getting new tyres and other spares was impossible. Sometimes, in bad weather, they had to walk three miles

[64]Margot Myers memoirs, translated by her daughter, Anne

to the village and back just to buy bread. In Paris, where her brother, Octave, was studying, even the children of Jewish families were being picked up.

In Lucenay, the occupying Germans were behaving reasonably well. Some people in the village even admired them. One woman told Margot perhaps the German victory would be a good thing. Another, that they had 'real class,' others said the Germans 'were not bad chaps.'[65] A few blamed the Jews for France's plight. Insidious propaganda was a regular feature of radio broadcasts, all of it pro-Pétain, some of it anti-Semitic. Margot was desperate to listen to the BBC to find out what was really happening. 'On French radio the voice of the old General Pétain, urging the French to submit to the Germans made my mother cry with rage. Only the BBC counted for her and many others from that day.'[66]

It was now more than four months since Margot had heard from her husband. Her only assumption was that if he had been killed in a bombing raid she would have been informed.

In his letters that were never posted, Geoffrey also exposed his anxiety about his mother, Rosetta. Short of funds and on her own, she was living in a hut in the garden of a cottage at Chinnor where she had taken refuge from the bombs raining down on London. Myers was relieved to be near her.

October 2 1940

Mother is still unwell. She says she is very lonely and may not have long to live. She says she is in despair over

[65]Margot Myers memoirs, translated by her daughter, Anne
[66]Memoir of Robert Myers with his sister, Anne

living alone. I hope she will keep her hut… The war is gradually and inexorably taking everybody in its grip. Every day another street is subjected to more terrors. The bombing also goes on in the country districts. Even the farmers in Chinnor look out for bombs. Three were dropped in the area this week. Not good for London women and children who had taken refuge in this village.

Mother told me of some friends of hers whose house had been bombed. The mother and father were downstairs. Their children, who were upstairs, were buried under the rubble of the explosion and killed. The parents were left to mourn.

While he was away from his squadron recovering from his car crash injuries, Myers wrote of his experiences in France and his escape at Dunkirk. In October, he returned to service with 257 Squadron and resumed his regular letters to his family about life in the Battle of Britain.

One of his first jobs after his return to duty was to visit David Hunt in hospital. His wife was virtually living in the hospital, giving her husband nursing care and support. Terry Hunt wrote, *'That night the door opened and in came the adjutant, and Geoff, the intelligence officer and dear David Coke whom we had not seen for stations and stations, since he landed his plane and was hurt. He held it up to show the place where his little finger had been and settled on the end of the bed… there was plenty of good talk that night, and we were all very cheerful. And Geoff, who always said the right thing, remarked that I was nursing on the front line which was a novel idea.'*

They talked about David's birthday party and Terry asked about Lancelot Mitchell, who she thought was the last surviving member of the squadron at the party, *'The adjutant cornered me in the corridor and fixed me with his pale eyes, and told me that Lancelot had just disappeared during a patrol. So now the party was indeed over.'*

Back at 257 Squadron, Bob Stanford Tuck was still leading from the front.

The Tuck legend rapidly grew. Twenty-seven swastikas were photographed on his plane and the newspapers spoke of the twenty-seven he had destroyed. It just happened that an overenthusiastic flight rigger had included the 'probables' and 'damaged' in the swastika score [Tuck's official list of victims was fourteen]. Tuck was photographed and filmed. He was described as the great ace of the war. The publicity did not affect his simplicity and sense of humour.

As intelligence officer Myers studied Tuck he began to understand him better. Tuck was determined and ruthless, 'a hard case,' as Larry Forrester put it, who 'would recognise only good and bad, strong and weak, truth and untruth, and had no time for in-betweens. A man whose mind was wondrously quick and clear, but not broad – a mind that could be at peace only with extremes, and couldn't cope with nuances.'

Myers understood that Tuck was ceaselessly trying to impress his father, for whom he was not the favourite son.

Tuck himself saw no room for sentimentality. 'The death of my close friend, Caesar Hull, had made me more tense than ever, more determined and ruthless with myself as well as with others. You couldn't think too much about the newcomers fresh from flying school.

They were pathetically surprised to find themselves killing or being killed.'[67]

Tuck told me that he was once the black sheep of the family. His father did not trust him and shook his head as he used to say 'that boy will come to a bad end.' Tuck's brother, a lieutenant in the tank brigade, was the hope of the family until he was taken prisoner near Dunkirk. At that time, Tuck was flying madly over Dunkirk, covering the great evacuation of the BEF from the sands into our little boats. He shot down several Ju 88s and Me 109s in that struggle. Over Dungeness a few weeks later he shot down a Ju 88 in a head-on attack. Those hawk's eyes of his found his mark. The Tuck legend began to grow from that time.

For all his heroics at Dunkirk it was still his brother – the tank lieutenant now a prisoner of war – who was the favoured son, even after Tuck's successes on Battle of Britain Day and all the attendant publicity for him, Immortal Tuck, the fighter ace.

Talking of his father Tuck said to me, 'the old man may be changing his ideas about me now. Up to recently he had nothing good to say for me and always talked of my brother... it'll shake him a bit now.'

Myers understood more about Tuck's complex relationship with his father when he discovered that, like himself, Tuck was Jewish. Forrester records, 'Geoff had a writer's habit of assessing and analysing character. He tried now to make a preliminary summing-up of Tuck:

"A brilliant flying record – fourteen kills...
fantastic luck and a series of incredible escapes...

[67]Interview with Author and Jane Nairac

reputedly a precise craftsman and incredible shot… a big drinker and party man, a tireless driving character who could go for days without sleep… an inspirer of men… tough and ruthless… deep down insecure about his father and obsessed by the trappings of success in an attempt to impress the old man."'

The adjutant, less a student of human nature than Myers, had been perplexed by the new squadron leader.

I thought of the adjutant's look of bewilderment when he spoke of Tuck. 'But he seems so foreign to me, Geoff,' he would say, opening his big, blue eyes unusually wide. Then he would pout a bit and mutter, 'I don't know but he seems more like a Mexican to me.' Tuck's brown face certainly had something Mexican about it. Sharp, sensual, cunning eyes, made to devour women or hunt down prey; dark, slightly wavy hair above his sloping forehead. Below his sharp nose, a little moustache cut well above his upper lip and slightly turned up; a small mouth. A film fan's idol, and something more behind.

Others in 257 took a more pragmatic view of Tuck and why he was such a success. Pete Brothers was clear.

Brothers knew what he was talking about when he said, 'Old Tuck is about the best shot in the Air Force. That's how he gets his stuff. I've seen him at target practice. There was no one to touch him.'

Myers grew to respect and admire his squadron leader but he was a careful, punctilious man and sometimes the claims of Tuck made him uncomfortable. 'Some pilots I knew had done their stuff, some had been shooting a line. Sometimes I had to check the ammunition to try to verify. It was difficult. With Tuck, line-shooting didn't matter compared to a man willing to take risks and inspire the squadron.'[68]

He was also ruthless when it came to pilots who let the RAF down. When, not long after he joined, Tuck saw two young sergeant pilots peel away from the action rather than engaging the enemy he was furious. His biography records, 'There was a white smouldering rage in the depth of his being. His eyes were vicious black pebbles. On the tarmac, he lifted his Mauser pistol and raised it at the two young pilots, saying, 'In time of war desertion is as bad as murder. Sometimes it is murder. It bloody nearly was today… you two deserve to be bloody well done! A bullet a piece – that's all your worth.'

He had the two men arrested. One was court-martialled and then demoted, last seen sweeping the control tower. The other, who had admitted his fault more honestly, was given a second chance and grew into a very capable pilot.

When he wasn't sorting out the remnants of 257 Squadron, Tuck flew from the front and his good fortune continued. Even the other pilots were amazed by what they called 'Tuck's luck'.

Tuck's luck became proverbial. He would go up on a weather test and come down after shooting a Ju 88 or a Dornier 17 into the sea. The difficulty for me as intelligence officer was to get confirmation. If a plane crashes into the sea, it usually sinks without leaving any traces behind. Tuck often said, 'Don't leave the bugger once you've got onto him. Hang on to him until you see him crash or the chaps bail out.' He used to describe

[68]Interview with Author

to us how he followed his own advice. In fact, after shooting down a Dornier or a Ju 88 single-handed into the sea, he would come back with such a wealth of detail that I was sometimes incredulous.

For an intelligence officer, accuracy was important but hard to achieve. A pilot might claim to have shot an enemy aircraft down but cloud or haze could have obscured the view. A Luftwaffe plane might be hit but could limp home to France instead of crashing into the sea. Collating successes in aerial combat was an inexact science. Stanford Tuck was obsessed with his own tally of 'kills'.

One day he asked me why I was so intent on getting the exact number of his combats and on compiling every detail. 'When you have shot down eighteen, recognised as destroyed,' I said, 'you will be ripe for the DSO.'

The next morning, he asked me for my records of his combats. He and I were alone at the dispersal point. I watched him sitting in an upright armchair by the fire with his feet on another chair and the file in his hands. His eyes seemed to be penetrating the paper, and his brain running under high-power... I was surprised at the long time Tuck spent pondering his score.

Despite Myers's cautious outlook on claims of 'kills' by Bob Stanford Tuck, he could see that Tuck was respected by his squadron. The two men developed a good personal relationship and, when a new boss arrived on the station, Tuck was positive about Myers.

The new station commander was pleased to find the fighter-hero in his mess and had a long talk with him. Tuck spoke about me. Afterwards, the station commander said to me, 'He's a splendid chap.'

So, to the RAF at large, and the wider public, Tuck was a hero, an ace, a film star. Myers saw this clearly when he was showing a fellow intelligence officer from 11 Group around the aerodrome.

He was proud to meet the great Immortal Tuck and to see him saunter out to his aeroplane to do a little local flying. As Tuck got into his plane, I said to him, half in a joke, 'Nice evening to bring one down. Cheer ho!' Before he landed forty minutes later, he shot up the aerodrome, diving down among the trees on the perimeter and zooming upwards a few feet above the dispersal hut. He was marvellous at aerobatics. As I watched him climb and roll in the sunlight, I thought I was looking at a swimmer revelling in the warm water of a clear lake. A slow roll to the right, and the ripples flowed down from the body of the plane, the billowing air caressed him and stroked the tips of his wings. Another dive in silence, and then the happy sound of the engine throbbing gently in the calm air.

As Tuck finally came into land, Myers was told via a call from operations that Tuck had shot an enemy aircraft down.

Tuck described the combat as a sporting journalist would a boxing match. He dictated his report to me, sometimes searching for several seconds to find the right adjective. He walked up and down the room, stopped by the fire, took a quick glance at a periodical lying on the table, and all the while went on dictating, 'I then gave him a forty second burst from 250 yards, closing to about 100 yards, seeing bits flying from his port engine. I dived below him and repeated my attack and… no, don't put that… say… made a similar attack from the starboard, firing two bursts of two seconds each. Return fire from the starboard gun was inaccurate. The enemy aircraft then dived into a cloud and I followed…

no… I succeeded in keeping on his tail and made a three-second burst from port as he emerged. This time I closed within fifty yards. One of the crew bailed out as the Dornier 17 dived slowly down to the sea and skimmed over the surface of the water. As I dived down to investigate, I noticed a last desperate attack before the plane hit the water and disappeared.'

Myers never denied Tuck's great skill, his gunnery expertise or his leadership but he had to smile at the Hollywood-scriptwriter style of his reports.

His combats usually had some outstanding feature which struck the popular imagination. In his combat reports he was particularly careful to polish the language describing the dramatic moments.

My colleague, who had not been with the squadron before, was thrilled at hearing the great war ace dictate his combat report. He was enthusiastic over the luck which had brought him down to the dispersal point just to see the air ace do a good piece of work. Tuck just smiled and brushed the compliments aside.

Peter Brothers was, in contrast perhaps, happy to share credit for 'kills'. 'What did it matter, I mean you gave away bits of your own score, but it built up the morale of the chaps you were leading.'[69]

Overall, the squadron were delighted to now be surrounded by success rather than failure. For those few who remembered the dark days of Squadron Leader Harkness this was a very welcome change. Tuck was not a man to leave 257 to their own devices because it was his day off. His leadership was quite the opposite.

[69]Nick Thomas, *Hurricane Squadron Ace* (Pen and Sword, 2014)

The boys were pleased at Tuck's luck and a little jealous that he always caught the German planes while they hardly ever saw any. They congratulated him as a matter of course. He took it all with a smile trying to assume modesty, and ordered a round of drinks.

The intelligence officer was a careful person. He respected Tuck and took notice of the positive views of Pete Brothers, but he also knew that it was his job to investigate and corroborate the claims of all pilots, even the Immortal Tuck. He did not want to give Group HQ incorrect information.

Before going up to the mess I checked up on Tuck's expenditure of ammunition. He had fired only 480 rounds, that is to say for about three seconds. In his combat report he had stated that he had fired for eleven seconds. It was a common mistake among less experienced pilots to imagine that they had fired three or four times as long as they did in reality... Nevertheless I was surprised that Tuck had so much overestimated the length of his bursts. He was usually more accurate.

Sometimes Tuck's fame was too exaggerated and overblown even for him.

I shall not forget his reactions to a full-page article which appeared in the *Daily Post* under the headline 'Tuck the Conqueror'. It described in rich, melodramatic journalese the conqueror's encounters with planes which, in point of fact, other members of his squadron had shot down. It depicted him succouring a dying airman whose last words were, 'I am happy to die under your leadership, sir. Keep this ring of mine. It will tell the world how you tried to save my life and it will preserve you from death.'

It described the sound of his machine guns as the voice of 10,000 typewriters rattling away at the same moment. The rest of it was in the same strain.

Tuck, by this time, was highly indignant that such a disgraceful piece of work should have got into the press.

The article's origins remained unresolved. The rumour in the mess was that one of Tuck's girlfriends had passed a few titbits on to the newspaper. Whatever the truth, none of this undermined Tuck's status as an ace. He continued with Tuck's luck, a series of solo kills out of nowhere.

Tuck went up with the squadron and was obliged to return just before they began chasing two unidentified aircraft. When he landed he said to me, 'I've just got an Me 109. It was a bit awkward, as I had no gun sights. My electric gear went unserviceable and that's why I left the squadron. I made a visual sign to Brothers to take over when I saw these two buggers coming at me. I made a tight turn and attacked the first one. I pumped for about six seconds in two or three short bursts and saw him spin into the drink. We were about half a mile away from the convoy, so they were bound to see the thing go in.'

Myers spent the morning trying to get confirmation of an enemy aircraft destroyed but none of the ships in the convoy had seen anything.

Looking back, it is easy to forget how young every pilot was. Even at the dizzy heights of Squadron Leader, Robert Stanford Tuck was just twenty-four, commanding a squadron of nineteen- and twenty-year-olds. According to his biographer, Tuck's future wife – Joyce – said after she met him a few months later, 'I was shaken when he told me he was just twenty-four. There were deep lines in his face and circles under his eyes. I wouldn't have thought he was a day under thirty.'

Pete Brothers was a superb foil to Tuck, and was thoughtful and honest.

That evening, Brothers and I talked over Tuck's exceptional series of individual victories. 'I've known him for several years,' Brothers said, 'and I have seen him do wizard things at shooting and aerobatics. He may shoot a line, too. Perhaps he embroiders a bit, but he wouldn't say that he had shot down anything if he had done nothing of the kind.'

Tuck was usually early into the bar and generous when it came to buying rounds for his weary squadron after a hard day in the air. The sergeants often partied in one place, and the officers in another. WAAF Corporal Daphne Wallis described social life at RAF Debden, where 257 had their forward base for much of the Battle of Britain. 'On the lighter side, during the Battle of Britain we used to get together, mostly on Sunday evenings, in the sergeants' mess. Most of the gathering were aircrew. Entrance was by invitation and we danced to our resident band made up of musicians in the famous bands of the 30s and [who] had played in the West End. The leader was Arthur Coppersmith. An older WAAF acted as chaperone, inspecting us before we went in, to see if any girl was wearing silk stockings – if so, she was sent back to the billet to change into regulation grey lisle ones.'

The social lives of the officers were more vivid. Or perhaps Myers, as a senior figure in the squadron, had closer insight into how they spent their time after taking on the Luftwaffe. Indeed, Tuck's luck appeared to extend to his private life. He drove as fast as he flew and attacked his social life with the same energy he showed in aerial combat.

The station adjutant has a mischievous and slightly ironical smile, weighs up everything he sees and is much brighter than he would have you believe. He said to me, 'He's a delightful fellow, but he's got the most vivid imagination – half of what he says seems to be pure fantasy.'

There was no stopping Bob Stanford Tuck. He had transformed a desolate and defeated squadron into a fighting unit that everyone could be proud to be a part of.

Tuck soon got his DSO. To celebrate, he gave a shilling's worth of free drinks and smokes to every member of the squadron. I never once heard him refer to this gesture, which cost him about ten pounds. It was natural for him to be generous, just as it was part of his nature to stick up for every member of his squadron and seize every opportunity to obtain advancement for them. He fought station commanders tooth and nail if he felt that his men were not getting a fair deal. 'I won't let the bastards get one over on me,' he would say. 'My squadron is going to be treated decently.'

Chapter Nine

October 14 1940

My Lovvy. My little Robert, My darling Anne,

The nightmare is continuing. I spent the evening in the anteroom of the mess, trying to forget things a bit. But it's no good. I can't. Others can. They drink, they listen to jazz, go to the cinema and really enjoy themselves. They have not got as much to remember. There's Pete Brothers downstairs, laughing with the other boys. The gramophone is playing dance tunes. Tomorrow or the next day they will go up and fight. Brothers is brave. I suppose his wife is in bed now, wondering, praying. Oh my Ducky, so are you.

Three weeks away from the war following his senseless car accident had given Geoffrey Myers time to think. In the heat of the Battle of Britain he had been busy every day collating intelligence information, supporting the young pilots in his squadron and trying to get Squadron Leader Harkness moved. In his time in hospital his thoughts, and his letters, had grown darker, more uncertain.

Ducky, I do hope you will see me again. I long to see you and my little ones. But if I am no longer here when the war is over, even if you are overtaken by disaster, keep your confidence in eternal things. What is happening now is beyond our grasp. In the order of things, after

centuries, which may be small spans of time in our lives here, and perhaps beyond, our torture of today may be the blessing of tomorrow.

There was nothing in the combat records of 257 Squadron to indicate why the mood of Myers should become darker and more reflective at this time. It was a relatively quiet period in the conflict. On October 12, three 257 Hurricanes were damaged by the Luftwaffe. Two pilot officers, Redman and Gundry, were shot down in the same morning combat over Deal but their Hurricanes were repairable. Ken Gundry was slightly wounded by shell splinters in the legs and thigh. In the afternoon, Carl Capon's plane was written off when he crashed at Stone in Kent, following combat with Me 109s over Dungeness. Capon was slightly wounded.

Although the skies over southern England were clearly still very dangerous, a month had passed since the heights of Battle of Britain Day on September 15. Hitler had started to turn away from plans for invasion. The relative calm gave Myers more time to write home.

Downstairs on the gramophone they've been playing, 'I can't love you anymore – anymore than I do now'. It all sounds so silly and the tune gets on my nerves. At the beginning of our seven years of married life the word 'love' meant something deeper for us than it did to most. But now, this conception has grown.

Your thoughts are my thoughts. Your life is my life. You are bound up in me. If we come together again, old age can but strengthen our intertwined branches. If we do not come together, I will still be with you, and the children will feel my presence through you. 'My Love,' when I breathe these words the tender parts within me throb, in harmony with you.

He also knew these pervasive and melancholy thoughts were not helping him, and he needed to get back to the job and to the reality of his life in Fighter Command.

He switched his attention back to the war going on around him in Suffolk and in the part of London where he had been brought up. Yet even these accounts were written through the prism of his relationship with Margot.

The German planes drop their bombs every night indiscriminately. Three nights ago, they dropped one on the maternity home in the neighbouring town. They dropped some in the fields nearby. Last night a block of flats in North London was destroyed and 200 people were buried and drowned through the bursting of a water main. Some of those 200 men and women were bound up in each other as you and I are. They were expecting to continue life together.

I have been lucky. Night after night they are wrecking parts of London. The poor city folk are bearing up despite the lack of sleep. The raiders are bombing the West End and the luxury flats as well as the East End slums. Thank goodness for that! We are all in it.

Direct contact with his family in France was impossible. The last message from Margot, passed via his journalist friends in Paris, had arrived as long ago as July – nearly four months earlier.

October 15 1940

My Ducky,

I did not go up to bed early tonight. They kept on dropping bombs around here, and it is more pleasant to be in company. I was talking tonight with Gundry about

the end of the war. Neither of us could see the end. Both of us have confidence. 'It does make one seek religion,' he said. 'One cannot imagine an evil system dominating the world.'

Throughout the Battle of Britain, Myers had tried to support his family by sending money to them. But, as contact with Margot and the children was so limited and infrequent, he had absolutely no idea if the money was reaching his family or not.

Cooks have written to me saying they are not satisfied that the money being transmitted by them to occupied France is reaching its destination so they are stopping payments for the time being. That is a blow to me. I wonder if you have received any of the money I sent through them?

'Conditions are good' – those four words in that message of July have made a great difference to my life, Darling. I feel that you are all right.

If I survive the war, it may be that you, my little children, will find a different Daddy from that of your imagination, and you may be disappointed. We would have to start at the beginning again, like new friends. If only they leave you alone.

In a second letter, written that same day, Myers shifts his focus back to the immediacy of the war.

This afternoon I wrote up the story of Mitchell's combats. He did not live long enough to qualify for the Distinguished Flying Cross. He was too reckless, poor boy! After I had taken out all the references of a secret nature, I shall send the account to his mother for her consolation.

After the initial news of Lancelot Mitchell's crash, his mother had written to the intelligence officer, clinging on to hope:

'You mentioned in your letter that it is not known whether he came down on land or water. Is it not possible that he could have been picked up at sea by some outgoing vessel? A friend of ours has sent us a message she received at a spiritualist meeting. She had taken my son's photograph... the medium's message was, 'This boy came down on water and is now safe but it will be weeks before you hear of him.' Now you will understand our very great hopes. This message had arrived in the midst of our great anxiety and sorrow.'

Geoffrey could understand the desperation of Mitchell's mother but was deeply distressed by the pain the Mitchells' family friend had thoughtlessly created by visiting a medium.

I am sure that Mitchell has gone... so the medium has raised false hopes. Poor Mrs Mitchell.

The main danger that Myers and the rest of the support staff in RAF Fighter Command faced was the continued bombing of British airfields. In the same letter of October 15 he reported:

I like being with you on these uncertain evenings. The bombers start flying over the aerodrome about seven o'clock and go on at irregular times all night.

Last night an unexploded bomb fell on the aerodrome and yellow flags have been placed all around it. I believe that it has buried itself too deep in the ground to explode. Other bombs dropped just outside the camp, near the station. An aeroplane is hovering overhead. I wonder

where the next bomb will drop. It does not matter much what I feel, because we are helpless anyway. Bomb-dodging is a joke until they come too near.

The randomness of the bomb-dropping was hard to fully comprehend.

'Look at poor old Ross,' Andrews, the bomb disposal officer, said, 'he was in one of the houses in the married quarters when they dropped their bombs all over the airfield. It was a hot day and he was resting on his bed stark naked. Before he knew it, he was thrown from his bed on the first floor out into the garden. The whole house was smashed in and he found himself bollocky naked, lying on his back in the garden. He grabbed hold of an old shirt, somebody else's pants and some slippers. Then he started working like a madman on the wreckage. We could see there was something queer about him… he had to be discharged from the service… shell shock and spine trouble.'

Myers wrote another letter to his wife in mid-October. This followed a visit from a journalist to the mess who had described the mass bomber attacks on the London Docks, and how he and other volunteers had worked through an inferno of flames on a salvage mission. On his way home he'd come across men digging in the remains of a shattered house. One of the men said:

'I've been working hard for the last three hours trying to bring out an old woman from the cellar of a house that had collapsed, and I don't know why, because it's my mother-in-law that's buried under there.' Finally, they made a small air hole and listened, 'Are you still alive, old girl?' someone

> **shouted through the hole. A feeble voice replied, 'I'm alive all right.' The men then split a bicycle tube open and made a funnel for pouring down milk. One said, 'Be careful, old girl, we're going to pour you down a little milk.' The feeble voice came up again through the hole, 'Make it beer.'**

The journalist from London used this story as a way of illustrating that the spirit of Londoners was so strong that defeat by the Germans would be impossible.

The German pilots go home and describe the military objectives that they've been hitting. We count up the wrecked churches and hospitals. They do the same in Berlin, after our bombing. London can become a place of desolation, so can Berlin. There's no way out of this nightmare but to go on. It's easy for me because I know what we are fighting for. But lots of the lads don't.

Under the leadership of Bob Stanford Tuck, 257 had turned dramatic failure into relative success. But the dangers of the aerial conflict had certainly not disappeared, even though the fire of the Battle of Britain was on its final embers. In his task of transforming 257 Squadron, Tuck was helped significantly by the arrival of Flight Lieutenant Peter Blatchford, a Canadian from Alberta, whose honesty and courage won immediate respect from the entire squadron. Blatchford was also hugely experienced, having enlisted in the RAF in 1936. But even with first-class leaders now at the helm, 257 – like several squadrons – still suffered losses on the afternoon of October 22.

Pilot Officer Norman Heywood from Cheshire was twenty-two. He had volunteered for Fighter Command only in August 1940, as the Battle of Britain really intensified. He had been with 257 for just eight days when he was killed by Britain's own defence armoury. The operational records written by Myers explained, 'While in combat with an Me 109 over Folkestone, he was killed by his own side and died near Lydd Church.'[70]

October 23 1940

Two more of our pilots were killed yesterday. I kept on hoping today, because no details of their deaths were available. But this afternoon we heard that one of them, Norman Heywood, a new pilot full of fun, had been shot down by our anti-aircraft defences at close range.

The second was twenty-year old Sergeant Pilot Bob Fraser. The two men were shot down within four minutes of each other over the Kent coast, although it seems that Sergeant Fraser lost his life in combat with an Me 109, unlike Heywood who had accidentally been shot down by British air defences. Fraser crashed and burned out at Moat Farm in Kent. The operations record book reported, 'about 12 Me 109s appeared and attacked the Squadron from behind and above. A dogfight took place.'[71] Myers wrote down his feelings about Sergeant Bob Fraser, who had been with 257 since the start.

I had come to believe that he would outlive the war. He had come back after so many of his fellow pilots had been shot down. He seemed to be so sturdy. Three weeks ago, he ran out of petrol and crashed in a field near the aerodrome. I raced to him on my bicycle and arrived at the same time as the ambulance. The poor lad had knocked out all his front teeth. His moustache was

[70]Battle of Britain Monument
[71]National Archives, Kew

not long enough to hide his disfigurement. His good-looking features were spoiled by the accident and he was acutely aware of this. He complained the other day that the dentist had not yet finished making his false teeth. Today, I suppose, the teeth were waiting for him.

Two days later, The Boy's Brigade in Glasgow wrote a letter of condolence to Mary, Bobbie Fraser's mother. 'The Prime Minister expressed not long ago the debt the whole country owed to those few gallant young men who saved the country from invasion. May we, the common people of the land, never forget what we owe to them. What would have happened to this land of ours had these young men not prepared themselves in advance it is difficult to realise. There was no murmur of complaint, no suggestions that the country was imposing on him. The hearts of many will go out to all of you in this tragic bereavement which has befallen you.'[72]

Bob Stanford Tuck recalled later, 'Telling a Sergeant Pilot's wife of his death was terrible but I understood more when I met the girl who was to be my own wife. It gave me the jitters every time I flew.'[73]

The deaths of Heywood and Fraser made Geoff Myers very uneasy too. He looked for comfort in his secret and private letters. On the day the pilots died, October 23, he wrote,

I should not write to you when I am feeling utterly miserable, My darling. I feel I should not depress you my little ones but when I am with you I feel less lonely. I am so utterly helpless. I can do nothing for you. My longing to see you is so great I must guard against it.

[72]Battle of Britain Monument
[73]Interview with Author and Jane Nairac

In this letter Geoff underlines that however much he was missing his family he was determined to win the war **which I realised before others, could not be avoided.** He was also acutely conscious that he was not on the front line.

I count those pilots that have disappeared and turn on myself saying 'You are still here. You have not shared their risks.' If I am called upon to play with death, I will do so Ducky, and you will know that I thought of you all.

Myers had a keen eye for the absurdities of service life but the inefficiencies also made him cross. Young men were risking their lives every day but even the RAF, to whom he was very loyal, continued to make mistakes. He had also seen plenty of laziness and time-serving when he was stationed in France in the Phoney War. This anger came to a head when Norman Heywood was needlessly shot down by his own air defences.

October 27 1940

There are still too many useless posts in the Air Force and in the Army. Up till now we had a very capable warrant officer with an efficient bomb disposal squad. Their work is to dig up unexploded bombs and render them harmless. Since bombs began to drop about the aerodrome they have been doing their work quietly and satisfactorily. Tonight, for no particular reason, an officer turned in the mess and said his job was bomb disposal. I asked him if he was an expert. He replied that he knew nothing at all about bombs but had come to look after the administrative side of bomb disposal. As if the administrative side of bomb disposal had not been attended to by the warrant officer!

Andrews, the bomb disposal warrant officer, laughed at this colossal waste of time and effort.

Then he told Geoffrey an even more absurd story of military hopelessness.

'Some weeks ago, a fellow came along to the mess and seemed to do nothing all day except drink like a fish. He said he was an "aerodrome discipline officer". He didn't know what the job was and it took him some days to make up his mind as to what he should do. He came to the conclusion the job must have something to do with flying, so he decided to tell the pilots when he thought they were taking off or landing carelessly. The pilots, of course, just laughed at him. So, he kept his mouth shut and went on drinking until he was found one day wandering aimlessly in Kent. They took him to a lunatic asylum. He had gone raving mad with the DTs.'[74]

The Battle of Britain was to come to its official conclusion at the end of October but there was still time for the squadron to suffer a final loss. On October 29, Sergeant Alexander 'Jock' Girdwood from Glasgow, who had been with 257 throughout the Battle of Britain, was killed at RAF North Weald. Pilot Officer Tom Neil from 249 Squadron, which shared the station at North Weald with 257, was a witness. 'A Hurricane, pointing west, sat outside our dispersal hut. On its belly and on fire. I hurried towards it to find Crossey and others standing beyond the circle of intense heat with their hands in their pockets. I peered through the smoke and flames. Not our code letters. Must be one of 257's. I turned to Crossey. Where was the pilot? A nod. Inside!'[75]

[74]Delirium tremens, severe shakes and confusion due to alcohol withdrawal
[75]Tom Neil, *Gun Button to Fire* (Amberley, 2011)

October 29 1940

My Love, My Children,

Sergeant Girdwood went this evening. I saw a great fire a few hundred yards away from our dispersal point. I didn't even know that he was in the middle of the fire. A few minutes before he went we were joking together. We just had to carry on as if nothing had happened. It was like that.

When Tuck heard how Sergeant Girdwood died, he looked down for a moment and thought. He said, almost under his breath, 'What tough luck.' Then he raised his head, flicked his fingers and said, 'Can't be helped. It's all in a day's work. There's a war on.'

22-year-old Jock Girdwood had joined 257 in May 1940 at RAF Hendon. He had survived virtually to the very end of the Battle of Britain. His friends and fellow sergeant pilots, Bobbie Fraser and Ronnie Forward, had joined on the same day. Jock Girdwood had taken off just as bombs were dropped on RAF North Weald in Essex where 257 had just been re-stationed. The legendary Major Adolf Galland led the escorting Luftwaffe aircraft that day. Girdwood had only just returned to 257 after having been shot down in August when he broke his foot. His plane was one of a flight of three Hurricanes – one flown by Squadron Leader Bob Stanford Tuck, the other by Polish Pilot Officer Francizek Surma – that had reached flight speed just when they were hit by the German bombs. Jock Girdwood's plane took the brunt of the blast.

Tom Neil continued to helplessly watch the Hurricane burning. 'It was like a funeral pyre. As the flames took hold, we watched a blackened and unrecognisable ball that was a human head sinking lower and lower into the well of the cockpit until, mercifully, it disappeared.

Then the fuel tanks gaped with whoofs of flame as the ammunition began to explode, causing us all to step back a pace, and the fuselage and wings began to bend and crumple in glowing agony. Finally, there was only the heat and crackling silence and ashes.'

It was really tough luck. Girdwood took off from the airfield just as the bomb dropped and blew him into the air. His plane, which must been hit by bomb splinters, crashed a few hundred yards away and burned furiously. We did not see this happening from our dispersal point because there were bombs dropping all over the airfield. We lay down in a ditch not more than three inches deep where they had put down a telephone wire. There had been no time to take cover.

Five of the ground staff were killed and about a dozen injured. It was a surprisingly small number for the twenty-seven bombs that dropped. Our good fortune.

The attack was beautifully planned and perfectly carried out. I take my hat off to those German pilots. They did their job properly.

Tuck knew he was very fortunate that his own luck had held and both he and his Hurricane were unscathed. He was a big fan of Polish pilots, all of whom were desperate to revenge the brutal annexation of their country by the Nazis. 257 Squadron had four Poles in its ranks. Tuck said, 'The Poles were utterly bloodthirsty. They wanted to kill all the time. When I stopped them flying for just a day they just stood on the runway and cried, tears rolled down their cheeks.'[76]

The day Jock Girdwood was killed, one of the Poles, Pilot Officer Francizek Surma, was lucky not to become

[76]Interview with Author

the seventh death in the bombing raid. He was flying at less than 1,500 feet when he was hit, but he still managed to bail out over the nearby village of Moreton. His Hurricane crashed in a rubbish dump to the south of the village.

His cockpit was a mass of smoke and his plane out of control when he jumped out. He landed in a treetop in the garden of an inn a few miles away. **When the innkeeper satisfied himself that he was a Pole and not a German he gave him two whiskies and soda.**

The story in the North Weald archives is more vivid. Surma was wearing a leather flying jacket with Nazi insignia on it, a trophy from an earlier wartime encounter. He was suspended above the ground in a line of elm trees. The North Weald archive adds, 'At this point two slightly different variations on his subsequent rescue exist. One, the least tasteful, has it that two French sailors climbed up to the helpless pilot and attempted to entangle his Germanic neck in the parachute shrouds, before help arrived. The second, acceptable, version of his rescue simply places two Dutch merchant seamen in the role of straight rescuers. When brought to the ground the worried Surma was whisked off to North Weald in a large Hispano Suiza sent to rescue him.'

In the notes written by Myers that evening, the intelligence officer made no mention of either French or Dutch sailors or, indeed, of Nazi insignia, despite what must have been a tempting story for a journalist like him.

Surma was lucky in more ways than one. Not having the correct uniform on could have been fatal. An interview with an anonymous pilot revealed a sad and grisly incident in the Battle of Britain. 'One man got shot down and bailed out. The fields were full of harvesting people and they killed him with pitchforks and farm implements. He didn't have a Royal Air Force suit on and he was chucking money down and papers to try and convince them who he was but they wouldn't have it. We took that very bad.'[77]

Flight Lieutenant Pete Brothers coped with the destruction caused by the brutality of the raid by trying to see the funny side of things. He was having tea in the mess when the raiders struck. 'We all dived under the table! My car, an open 3-litre Bentley, was parked outside and I was livid to find the near-miss bomb had filled it with soil, which took forever to clean out.'[78]

The bomb disposal warrant officer, Andrews, took a similar approach – describing, to much laughter, how a new aircraft hand reported for duty.

The chap went to report at the adjutant's office explaining, 'I started to report at the guardroom, sir, but it's no longer there.'

Tom Neil from 249 recorded, 'A number of 257's ground staff had also been killed and others wounded and a Polish officer of theirs had been forced to bail out.'[79] The overall damage to the aerodrome and all the squadrons stationed there was far worse. The German raid left nineteen dead and forty-two wounded. Five of the casualties were from 257 squadron.

Later, Pilot Officer Tom Neil reflected on what he had seen and felt, 'I retired that night more than a little concerned that I had treated the cremation of 257's chap

[77]Joshua Levine, *Forgotten Voices* (Ebury Press, 2006)
[78]Nick Thomas, Hurricane Squadron Ace (Pen and Sword, 2014)
[79]Tom Neil, *Gun Button to Fire* (Amberley, 2011)

so lightly. What on earth was coming over me? I had watched a colleague burned to a cinder and had felt… well… almost nothing. Not like me at all. Downright worrying, in fact.'

Although 257 did not know it then, October 30 was later determined as the end date of the Battle of Britain. In that context, Sergeant Jock Girdwood was the final 257 pilot to die in the Battle of Britain, just twenty-four hours before its official end.

Chapter Ten

Fighter Command had been victorious in the Battle of Britain simply by virtue of not being beaten. Hitler no longer planned to invade Britain nor did he expect that his air force would inflict so much damage that Britain would sue for peace. Hitler turned his attentions elsewhere. The heroic defensive courage of the young fighter pilots had been crucially helped by the skilful use of radar and other intelligence work, including that of the Observer Corps. The Germans had made mistakes, shifting attacks to London just when their airfield bombing strategy was starting to bear fruit. They consistently underestimated the strength and resilience of Fighter Command. As Pete Brothers put it in his biography, 'The winter was coming and clearly there was not going to be an invasion. The Battle of Britain had been won.'

But for 257 Squadron, the war, rather than the battle, was far from finished. Bombs were still being dropped, convoys still needed to be protected and danger was still high. For Geoffrey Myers, his family situation was unchanged. His wife and two children were still trapped in occupied France and stories about Jews being persecuted or rounded up grew in frequency. His desperation to smuggle his family out of the occupied zone, across the border to unoccupied territory and down to Spain or Portugal, intensified. It was an escape plan fraught with danger.

In October 1940, Philippe Pétain passed a restrictive Jewish statute but already the 150,000 Jews who had travelled south to escape the Nazis had apprehended the discrimination against them in the so-called free zone too. The statute banned Jews from public posts and some jobs. The collaborationist policies of Pétain meant that, between 1940 and 1943, the Vichy government was implicated in the transportation of Jews to concentration camps. Overall, of the 76,000 Jews from France sent to Auschwitz and other camps in the war, fewer than 3,000 returned alive.

Myers was still trying to send money to his family and, through his friends and journalistic contacts, find an escape route for Margot and the children. He sent messages to his family through his friends – the Renards, in Clermont-Ferrand – but he had no idea whether those messages, or any money, was reaching his family in Lucenay-lès-Aix. In return, he had heard nothing from France since July, over three months earlier.

November 2 1940

My Ducky,

I wrote to you last night through our friend telling you that I could not send you any money. I was afraid that you might receive the two monthly instalments that I sent through Cooks and then expect others to follow. Perhaps I may hear that the arrangement has been resumed. I would prefer you to get even a few shillings out of the ten pounds than nothing at all. But I have no choice. Payments have been stopped.

In France the Guimiot family was focused on survival. They worked the fields, raised chickens and rabbits and killed a pig. There was no petrol and the family relied on a little donkey cart and horse wagon. Margot's thoughts, however, were centred on what to do next. 'I was becoming more and more worried. I felt danger approaching. England was still resisting. Should I try to pass into the free zone? I knew that freedom was only a relative thing, but perhaps all the same it would be safer there.'[80]

Myers had been on a visit to see his mother, Rosetta, and it brought back memories of happier times.

Only fourteen months ago you were in this house in Furzedown Road with Robert and me. I could see you at the dinner table. Your presence, and your little presence, Robert, filled the rooms. When I play with little children I half play with you, Robert and Anne. And I long for you.

He went with his mother on a visit to the countryside but, to him, the cottage they were in was an unhappy place.

We were in the cottage which recently belonged to a woman who left for America with her children. She went because her husband is a prisoner of war in Germany and her parents were in the United States. She left probably thinking that her husband would feel more at ease if he knew her to be in America. She and her family went down in a boat in the Mid-Atlantic. The man's fate haunted me in the cottage. I was lucky compared with so many others.

[80]Memoirs of Margot Myers translated by her daughter, Anne

Myers's colleagues in the squadron tried to persuade him to join them at a dance but his thoughts were too much with his family

November 9 1940

But they did not insist because they know that when I wanted to stay in alone, my thoughts are dancing with you, dancing over the meadow at Beaurepaire, down to the stream where the watercress grows, to the river where the white cows stand under the oaks. The boys are enjoying the dance. Oh how I adore you my Luvvie.

Eventually, after many months of unnerving silence, Myers received news that his family were alive in France. He also learnt that Margot's brother, who had joined the French forces at the start of the war and been captured by the Germans, was a prisoner in Germany. But at least he was alive.

November 18 1940

For hours last night I was trying to write a letter to you. I have received news of you through Portugal but this was tempered by a feeling of guilt that I have messed things up. I should have tried more ways to get in touch with you. Perhaps some of my messages have reached you at last and you are no longer anxious. What would be the good of raising your hopes too much?

I must tell you about Peter Blatchford tonight. He is not the tall fair-haired hero who appears in little boy's dreams. He is stocky, thickset with a big head well planted on his body. Dark silky hair brushed back above a broad forehead. The whole is a setting for eyes that glint strength, and diffuse tenderness. His movements, like his eyes, are sometimes so swift that they surprise

onlookers. Usually they are gentle and a natural dignity accompanies them. The first time I saw him I said to myself, 'that is a man whom I shall like and respect.'

In fact, Peter Blatchford's given name was Howard but he preferred to be called Peter. Inevitably too, given his roots in Alberta, Blatchford was often called Cowboy. This was Bob Stanford Tuck's favourite name for him, although he occasionally called him Fat Arse. In turn, Blatchford called Tuck Beaky. The two superb pilots had great mutual respect for each other.

In Tuck's biography, Cowboy is described affectionately. 'He was cheery-faced, chunky and chuckle-voiced with an extraordinary large backside that made him waddle and roll like an overfed puppy. The slowness of his movements and mannerisms proved wholly deceptive – his mind was rapier-swift, his reflexes instantaneous. He was a brilliant shot, never got excited – all told, a natural.'

Tonight, Blatchford had too much to drink. He remained responsible for his movements but not always his words. 'Come on, Geoff, and have a drink,' he said to me before dinner, taking me by the arm. He, Tuck and the pilots had been celebrating the birth of Pete Brothers's daughter. They were on their third bottle of champagne and had been having stronger drinks earlier in the day. He had been doing all the heavy lifting in the squadron for the last three weeks. Stanford Tuck had been letting things slide and Brothers had had several grants of special leave. It was always Blatchford who did the organising, checked the state of the aeroplanes and shouldered responsibility for everything that went on in the squadron.

Blatchford had hitherto had no glory. Three times he had come back from air battles and made no claims.

I know others in the squadron who would have made out a good case for having at least damaged an enemy. Blatchford would not stoop to that sort of thing if there was the slightest doubt in his mind. His courage was natural.

Three weeks before, Blatchford was almost blown out of the sky by cannon from a 109. He went on fighting with a huge rent in his fuselage and petrol streaming out from under his aircraft.

He treated the whole thing as a joke. Blatchford bent down and swung his arms quickly to show me the movements of the planes. Those dark vivacious eyes of his followed the movements of his arms until the pupils, like little stars, were shining through the corners of their windows.

On November 11 1940, Blatchford became a popular hero when he led the squadron on a dull convoy patrol over the east coast. For the first time, Italian planes came to attack the RAF. They had almost no involvement in the aerial war over Britain thus far, but Mussolini had insisted in helping the Luftwaffe. The Italian pilots were brave but their Fiat CR.42 biplanes and Fiat BR.20 bombers were no match for the speed and firepower of the Hurricanes and Spitfires from Fighter Command.

Jonathan Reeve used Blatchford's own words to describe what happened.

'I must say that the Italians, as they turned out to be, stood up to it very well. I singled out one of the enemy and gave him a burst. Immediately he went straight up into a loop. I followed him when he suddenly went down into a vertical dive. I still followed, waiting for him to pull out. Then I saw a black dot move away from him and a puff like a white mushroom – someone bailing out. The next second the bomber seemed to start crumpling up and it suddenly burst into hundreds of small pieces. They fell down to sea like a snowstorm. I must have killed the pilot. I think he fell back, pulling the stick with him. That's what caused the loop. Then he probably slumped forwards, putting the plane into an uncontrollable dive.'[81]

Then, Cowboy Blatchford spotted more bombers who were mixed up in the sky and were streaming smoke. He continued:

> 'At that moment another one shot past me flaming like a torch, and plunged into the sea. I saw a dogfight going on above with another type of aircraft I had never seen before. They were Fiat fighter biplanes. There must have been about twenty of them milling around with the Hurricanes.'

Although underpowered, the Fiats were very manoeuvrable and Cowboy soon found himself in a sustained battle with one Italian fighter.

'It was a long dogfight, as dogfights go. We did tight turns, climbing turns and half-rolls till it seemed we would never stop. Neither of us was getting anywhere until one of my bursts seem to hit him and he started waffling. For a moment he looked completely out of control. I got in two or three more bursts and then ran out of ammunition. That put me in a bit of a fix and I didn't know what to do next… then he straightened up – he was just thirty yards ahead and I was a few feet

[81]Jonathan Reeve, *Battle of Britain Voices* (Amberley, 2015)

above. At that moment I decided that, as I could not shoot him down, I would try and knock him out of the sky with my airplane. I went kind of haywire.'

Although Peter Blatchford had lost up to nine inches from both his propellers, and later found them splattered with blood, that did not stop the Canadian. With no ammunition, he launched a dummy head-on attack on two more Italian planes which promptly turned tail and fled. Myers was away from the squadron that day but recorded the event in a letter home in his notebook.

November 18 1940

The RAF pilots pounced on the bombers and pumped their ammunition into them. Then they punished the Italian fighter protection planes. Three of the Italian planes came to grief on land, several others crashed into the sea. Blatchford got so excited when he had finished his ammunition he swept right into one of the Italian planes, smashing the end of his own propeller and the Italian's as well. The intelligence officer who was deputising for me described how the acting Squadron Leader 'rammed' the enemy plane.

As the operations record book concluded, 'F/Lt Blatchford, on running out of ammunition, attacked a fighter by ramming it, milling the enemy aircraft's main top wing with his propeller. Two blades of F/Lt Blatchford's propeller were damaged. The squadron got two crests off the crashed bomber which was at Woodbridge and a bayonet sheath and two steel helmets as trophies.'[82]

[82]National Archives, Kew

Polish pilot, Karl Pniak, played his full part. According to Sergeant Pilot Reg Nutter, Pilot Officer Pniak 'forced one of the bombers to surrender.' [83] This was indicated to him by the upper rear gunner who stood up in his turret with his hands above his head. 'He [Pniak] attempted to guide the aircraft to Martlesham but the Italian made a crash-landing near Woodbridge, Suffolk.'

As Blatchford put it, 'I was a bit worried because my plane had begun to vibrate badly, but I managed to land all right. Just as I got out of my Hurricane and was walking away, my fitter and rigger ran after me saying that I had six inches missing from one of my propeller blades and nine inches from another. All the same, it was certainly a grand day for the squadron.'[84]

In his notebook, Geoff continued, **For the next few days the wireless, press and the films were full of the squadron's action. Our pilots were photographed with bottles of chianti, crests, Finn hats, daggers and other spoils taken from the Italian planes. Peter Blatchford is to talk on the wireless of his exploits. The speech has been prepared with the aid of a press officer. Soon, I hope, Peter will get a Distinguished Flying Cross.**

On November 17, six days after the vanquishing of the Italians, Blatchford hit another Messerschmitt in a minor skirmish. South-east of Harwich he opened fire on the leading 109 but as he levelled out, he saw a Hurricane flown by Sergeant Bernard Henson across right in front of the smoking 109. The damaged German fired into the easy target, sending Sergeant Henson toppling down towards the ground. His Hurricane was

[83]Battle of Britain Monument

[84]Jonathan Reeve, *Battle of Britain Voices* (Amberley, 2015)

seen to hit Lighthouse Sunk, a sandbar off Harwich. It was not until January 1941 that Henson's body was washed ashore miles away, near Dover in Kent.

We tried to slur over the battle and went on hoping that Sergeant Henson would turn up. This evening there was no longer any hope. The action remained on Blatchford's mind. It was as if the film of the battle was repeated over and over before his eyes.

He said, 'I know you understand, Geoff. It's not the Italian business but this. I saw Sergeant Henson go down. He did not appear to be crashing but was gliding down in gentle circles with smoke pouring out. I thought he would get away with it.'

After the German had shot down Bernard Henson, Blatchford had not hesitated to chase the limping 109.

'When I shot at that pilot,' he went on to say, 'his Me 109 started belching smoke. I was chasing him… I closed in and got within fifty yards. Then he suddenly put out his arm and looked at me as if to say 'Don't fire'. But I pressed the button and the Messerschmitt crashed into the sea. He was thrown out and then I saw him for a moment stretched out on the water. Then he disappeared. He must have been dead when he fell out of the plane as it crashed. He was a tough guy, Geoff, a stout fellow. I didn't want to kill him. I've been thinking about it all the time.

Peter screwed up his eyes slightly and pulled up his shoulders to give himself poise. 'I'm not a killer, Geoff,' he said, looking straight into my eyes. 'I don't like it. I just do it because I've got to.' He hesitated and continued to hold my eyes in his.

He must have seen something in my eyes. 'No Geoff,' he said, 'I won't let it get me down. No, I won't do that. I promise you that.'

The two men had another drink but the incident was still on Blatchford's mind.

'Maybe he might have jumped and bailed out, Geoff, if I hadn't shot the second time. Perhaps he would have been picked up by a boat. I was so excited, I just pressed the button.' I tried to talk but couldn't. 'Oh Geoff,' he said, 'my dream is to bring down a great big bomber, with all the men on board, and just have them as prisoners. I am not a killer.'

He raised a smile. 'I like Germany,' he continued, 'I liked the people I met there. You know, Geoff, I went to a German school at home and learned quite a lot of the language. I can understand what they say. I had a good Canadian-German friend, a butcher called Otto Sass. I used to go behind the counter in his butcher shop when I was a boy and loved it. He was a fine man. He was a good Canadian but loved his home.

That evening, Cowboy Blatchford continued to drink as a pheasant shot by one of his fellow pilots, the Hon. David Coke, was passed round.

Blatchford picked up a leg with his fingers and bit into it. 'We're not at a dinner party,' he said, 'we can eat pheasant properly.' He enjoyed his pheasant and enjoyed drinking champagne with it... he put down his glass and that special smile of his played round his lips.

Myers had the melancholy duty of packing up the belongings of Bernard Henson. He wrote a letter to his wife in France down in his notebook.

November 18 1940

I packed Sergeant Henson's belongings this evening. Sergeant Deash, who was previously in the same

squadron as he, and was posted here with him, helped me to go through his papers. They had been sharing a room since we arrived here. Deash is now the only sergeant left in A Flight. His three companions were shot down during the last three weeks. He does not feel he can carry on. He would like to apply for an instructor's post. He wants to get away from here but nothing can be done about it.

'We must go through his letters carefully,' Sergeant Deash said, with a wicked little grin on his face which meant, of course, further explanation is unnecessary.

The first letters were from Henson's wife.

'They had been married for three years now,' Deash said. 'She loved him very much. The curious thing was that he wrote to her every day… she's expecting a baby in about two months,' said Sergeant Deash as he put the letters on the pile of correspondence to be returned to her.

A different handwriting. We looked at the last words, 'your loving Mother,' and the words before the end, 'May God preserve you, my Dear Son.'

That was not the end of the letters.

The next letter was in round, schoolgirlish characters and was signed Violet. It was on pink paper. 'That one goes on the fire,' Deash said with a decisive nod '… she's a WAAF. Saucy girl. They carried on together at the Nine Gates Inn and he wangled a room for them there. He may have put her in the family way too.'

The next letter involved a third woman.

The next letter I took up gave substance to Sergeant Deash's remark. It was from a solicitor and read: 'Dear Sir, The case will come before the court next Thursday. I take it from your letter of the 19th instant that you have decided to admit paternity…'

'That's another woman,' Sergeant Deash said. 'He told me he was in a bit of a fix about her, but I didn't know she had taken the case to court.'

We went on sifting. One or two unpaid bills. A powder puff. Secret instructions on Very High Frequency Wireless for Fighter Aircraft. More letters from his wife.

We went on sorting. Letters from Eleanor, from May, from Tilly, WAAFs and girls outside every aerodrome. It seemed improbable that our sorting and sifting would do much good. Perhaps the court case would not be heard now that he was missing. Even if it were heard and the woman won, she would only get a few shillings from the widow's pension.

Nonetheless, the two men continued to look through the dead sergeant's belongings. Myers was conscious of his wish to protect the pregnant wife as best he could.

We emptied the suitcase and shook it. Just as I was about to close it, a photograph the size of my thumbnail fluttered out. It was of a girl in a bathing dress. Her bosoms were exposed above the dress which was cut to allow a band of flesh and her navel to be on view. I was struck by the girl's broad mouth and sensual, vulgar laugh.

In the Battle of Britain everything speeded up, including relationships. Young men grabbed at pleasure because they knew that they might not be alive the next day. Women did not know if a man they liked and had hopes for would be around much longer. That same evening, Squadron Leader Stanford Tuck had shown up at the mess where, over a few drinks, Blatchford and Myers had been rerunning both Sergeant Henson's death and the shooting down by Blatchford of the German pilot.

We jumped into the squadron car. Tuck drove us over to Woodbridge, to the Crown and Anchor. On the way we sang the songs that the RAF enjoy. I won't repeat them.

A pilot from another squadron was giving a party because he was getting married in two days' time.

Drinks all round. The pilot's eyes were bleary already. Getting married was just like bringing down a Gerry plane to him. Just another bit of adventure.

The soon-to-be married pilot, who had a DFC and had distinguished himself in the Battle of Britain, was pouring drinks rapidly.

'Have another drink, old boy. I'm getting married. Ha! Ha!'

Myers looked round for Tuck, wanting a lift home in the squadron car Tuck had driven them to the pub in.

Tuck had disappeared. Women were sometimes more important than drinks. A luscious body, a soft bosom, a comfortable bed. The juice of life. A beer afterwards. A night drive, a thick head in the morning. Clear it with a few aerobatics and a good sniff of oxygen. 'Where's Tuck?' someone asked… The pilots looked doubtfully at the womenfolk. The womenfolk giggled and tittered.

The rest of the pilots continued to drink.

Pete Brothers came up to me with a half-filled glass dangling in his fingers. 'Absolutely sozzled. Whistled as a coot. Shozzled…' he said, swinging from side to side and gracefully waving his first finger in circles as if it were a plane evading a German attack. 'Absolutely sozzled-sozzled. Thanks Geoff, I'd have spilled the lot on the carpet. You saved it.' I had rescued his glass. 'Take me home, Geoff. I must get out of here or I won't be able to get home. Ha! Ha!'

I got him out of the inn and into his Bentley sports car. The cold air steadied him. After cracking a mudguard against the wall of the courtyard he sobered up and drove the five miles back at high speed. Sitting by his side, I expected at every turn of the road to end up in a ditch. I was limp with fear and could not remember the password to enter the aerodrome.

In December 1940, Cowboy Blatchford was awarded the Distinguished Flying Cross. The citation read, 'In November 1940 this officer was the leader of a squadron which destroyed eight and damaged a further five enemy aircraft in one day. In the course of the combat he rammed and damaged a hostile fighter when his ammunition was expended, and then made two determined head-on feint attacks on enemy fighters, which drove them off. He has shown magnificent leadership and outstanding courage.'[85]

[85] *London Gazette*, December 1940

Chapter Eleven

Even if the Battle of Britain was at an end, the danger for the young pilots of Fighter Command was not over. The war had nearly four more years to run and, although Hitler had abandoned plans to invade, Britain was still at war with Germany and attacks were frequent. For the Myers family, occupied France was dangerous too, with informers only too ready to identify Jewish children to their Nazi occupiers.

November 30 1940

For the last few days I have found it more difficult than usual to be jolly. I have been with you at Beaurepaire, trying to imagine your daily life, failing, and then have been prey to doubts and fears. I keep on feeling that perhaps I have not done something which I might have done but I don't know what it is.

My Love, I would not lose those wonderful seven years of our married life, even if I knew beforehand that I would suffer afterwards. The thought of you keeps me going. I adore you. I long to see you and my little ones. But there is no horizon.

Myers still had plenty of work to do as intelligence officer, supporting 257 and listening to the pilots' problems, both professional and personal. A Polish pilot from the neighbouring squadron – with whom 257 shared the aerodrome – was angry at being overlooked for promotion. So on the same day Geoff wrote a second letter to his wife that was to be read after the war.

Seeing me in the chair opposite, or rather, somebody in a chair opposite he said, 'Have a drink.' He would not hear of a refusal. We would all get drunk together. 'You may think me sissy,' he said, 'but I'm fucking annoyed – furious in fact. They've just had a bloody twerp of a flight lieutenant posted to the squadron when I've been leading the flight for three months. You'll think it is a bloody line I'm shooting but I'm not... Of the last seventy sorties I have led fifty, not the flight but the whole fucking squadron... It's because I'm a foreigner that they won't have me as flight commander. Why did they give me a DFC?

Myers tried to reason with the pilot, pointing to other pilots from overseas who were leading flights or squadrons. But it was to no avail.

'I could cry with rage,' he said, stamping his foot and taking another gulp of gin. He screwed up his eyes and stamped, 'It took me three bloody years to become a fighter pilot and now I'm going to be posted as a bomber, because I won't stand for this. Have another drink. I'm drunk already. If I stay on as a fighter pilot, I'll shoot down our own pilots. I'm brassed off.'

As the Pole continued to drink the real reason for his concern and anger began to emerge.

He sprawled in the armchair. The uncertain look which entered his weak, dreamy eyes, fluttered around the room. The words that came out of his mouth continued to make sense, 'I need the extra pay... I'll soon be having a kid. I've got to keep the wife going. I need the extra pay.'

Myers sought out reassurance from his fellow intelligence officer from the Polish pilot's squadron. The man told him with a laugh,

'Take no notice of him… he gets easily depressed, but he's all right the next day. He may think he's led the squadron, but he hasn't. He'll be all right tomorrow if you leave him alone.'

Drinking was still the chosen means of escape from wartime pressures. One day, Geoff and the squadron had a visit from the senior staff at the local searchlight post. Drinking moved from the mess to the back room of a local inn and, initially at least, the conversation was serious as the men discussed the politics of a post-war world.

December 1 1940

The usual round of drinks started. Double whiskies, sherries, half cans… one of the searchlight lieutenants said, 'Of course, you've got to cut Germany up into small states again, but you can't let them start building another army as soon as the war is over. Sterilise all the men is what I say. Do what they've been doing in their own country. It's a much less painful method than killing them off. It is they who have brought all this misery and ruin on Europe. Sterilise the bastards, I say.'

I said that this suggestion filled me with disgust. There seemed to be no point in fighting if we were prepared to adopt Nazi methods after the war. Others agreed.

The night continued more merrily after that conversation and Geoff's friend in the searchlight unit, Charlie, led the way.

Charlie stiffened up. He was at his eleventh or twelfth double whisky –a little more than usual and it began to tell.

With Pete Brothers at the wheel and Carl Capon alongside, the drunken Charlie decided to play a joke. After the men had stopped to relieve themselves by the roadside he pretended to collapse in the road. Pete Brothers drove slowly on knowing that Charlie was playing the fool and would soon catch up. Soon, Charlie was out of sight when a big Army lorry came round the bend.

Charlie was lying all crumpled up in the middle of the road and panting heavily. Half groaning, half crying he said, 'Oh Geoff, the lorry. Oh, it's not a joke... the lorry... lay down, didn't hear it... ran me over.' He spoke slowly and faintly, gasped again and went on groaning. 'I felt as if somebody had tried to strangle me...' I took hold of Charlie's hand.

The utter futility of the whole thing flashed through my mind. A night at an inn. Overdrinking. He must have fallen asleep after lying down in the road. Charlie's hand was limp, but still warm as he moaned and gasped again. I was beside myself. Suddenly his hand stiffened and gave mine a good squeeze. 'You bastard,' I shouted. Charlie guffawed...

While Myers was dutifully writing his experiences and thoughts in his notebooks, in occupied France, Margot Myers had not heard from her husband in England for nearly six months.

December 6 1940

I am waiting for every mail in the hope of receiving another word about you. Just a word to reassure me. I am also waiting for news of the family in Southampton after the devastating bombing there.

I hope you do not listen to the French wireless. The propaganda of the Paris radio is unsettling. I must not think of France. Let me just think of the past.

December 12 1940

The squadron was first moved to the north of England. Killed, missing and posted have accounted for all the officers but the doctor and two pilots. 257 was then moved south again, back to East Anglia, and closer to the front line.

December 18 1940

We have now been at Coltishall for little more than a week. Our pilots call it the Bullshit and Bumff Station. Obligatory church parades, a fat volume of standing orders, a mess like a morgue and stiff plots of grass around roads with one-way traffic... a station where fighter pilots are apt to feel they are of secondary importance in comparison with the overwhelming number of portly gentlemen who comprise the ground staff officers.

We arrived for Christmas. Plenty of good fun, hemmed in by regulations. The WAAFs, who had been over-disciplined for months, went wild, got drunk and lolled around the place kissing officers and men indiscriminately... all because the regulations were applied so rigorously, to give the impression that the place was spotless.

We arrived here feeling depressed, so we were naturally prejudiced against the place from the start. Pete Brothers was posted from the squadron. He was sent off to be an instructor at an operational training unit... Two others went off at the same time as Pete,

then two days after we had moved here, five more of the pilots were posted. The squadron has been torn to shreds. Peter Blatchford is still here. If he goes there will be nothing left.

Brothers had already turned down one promotion to stay with his squadron until he felt that his job was done. Myers, too, refused a promotion. He was asked by the station commander at North Weald, a man he hugely respected, to become intelligence officer for the whole station rather than just a single squadron.

I would have liked to serve under him but my heart was with the squadron. I ought to have guessed that it would change again as much as it did during the first phase of the long weeks of the battle.

In hospital, Pilot Officer David Hunt was recovering slowly from further operations on his burns, as his wife recorded in her book. *'He was lying there in the big ward where they had moved him. There were blood spots below the crepe bandages over his eyes. He told me that everything had gone to schedule and that he should be home by Christmas. David panicked sometimes behind his bandages. He said it was like that moment in blind man's bluff when you are suddenly aware of the darkness, and you must tear off the bandages or suffocate. I hated to leave him in his blindness each day at four.*

'The purple mask was coming off all the time. The nurse would cut curved strips off it with scissors, and soon there was nothing left but a false nose; a fascinating object, so loose round the edges that you longed all the time to lift it off. It seemed quite natural to have a husband with a purple false nose; and it was only when

the nurses were there that I stood back and called him koala...'

With Brothers and so many others gone, Myers wondered how the squadron would hang together and what the impact would be on some of the younger pilots.

Carl Capon will not want to stay in a training squadron, even though he has been with us from the beginning. He is no longer shy in the mess. He is glad to find that he can drink double whiskies and be at readiness the next morning. To give himself more confidence, he has taken to criticising the food, the servants and the service as a whole. His criticisms are made in a gentle way... He will never really grow old as long as his golden hair curls slightly over his clean forehead and blue, bashful eyes. Capon is one of the few unmarried pilots who never talk loosely about women. He is chaste. When he goes home it is always to visit 'Pop, Mum and the little brother.'

He often talked to Myers about his worries, especially what he would do after the war. Myers always tried to boost Capon's confidence, to let him know that his skills and judicious sense of right and wrong would serve him in good stead whatever came next.

He was direct in his speech, clean in everything. His personal affairs were always in order, his laundry placed neatly in his drawers, his post office savings book had a substantial credit. He had become our favourite. I teased him by calling him our mascot. In fact, I always teased him. Tuck had recommended him for a mention in dispatches.

As Christmas drew closer, Myers naturally thought more and more of his family and, once again, he grew gloomy.

December 20 1940

My Ducky, My Little Ones,

Tonight I happened to look into the mirror and saw an old man. He had a scar on his forehead, wrinkles below and sad, tired eyes. His hair was still dark and he had a trimmed moustache but both might have been grey. He looked as if his thoughts were either a long way away or wandering into the past. He was therefore an old man. Those drooping eyebrows must be an indication of sorrow. 'Not a cheerful companion,' I thought. 'He should pull himself together, not let the gloom get the better of him. He should be stronger, think of the future and be confident. He should be brave.'

I did not recognise myself. I had to move my head, just to convince myself that it was I.

Myers found the forced jollity of the wartime RAF difficult. He was, by nature, a serious-minded man with deep feelings. He was also more than ten years older than most of the squadron and had a family in France which set him apart. But he also knew that being jolly was part of his job – a way that he could support his pilots, listening to them over a whisky or heading off to the pub with them. But clearly, he didn't like it.

December 31 1940

My Ducky, my little children,

New Year's Eve is over. I went to the sergeants' mess. I tried to shake off my feelings and forebodings. I tried to be jolly but I could not dance. I have got to hate the sight of flirting women. The WAAFs fill me with disgust and scorn when they throw away restraint so easily.

The adjutant, Freddie, encouraged me. He hinted that I should force myself to be jolly. I knew he was right.

I made an effort. I chatted foolishly, laughed and told jokes. I tried to be social and drank plenty of whiskies and beer. Freddie danced, bumped into me with a WAAF. I took the hint, danced, and was furious. I don't know what she looked like. I was wondering all the time if I should force myself to dance like this. In the end, I said to myself 'Damn it, no. Either be at ease and make others jolly or don't attempt anything.'

When we got back to the officers' mess, Freddie stayed up and played bridge, snooker or poker until four o'clock in the morning. Tomorrow he will not be up in time. Happy New Year! I'm off to bed.

Geoffrey Myers was right. Ernie did not get up in time for the first day of 1941. Five new sergeant pilots had arrived and Bob Stanford Tuck asked Myers to put them through their paces.

January 1 1941

Happy New Year. Good God! What a start.

Stanford Tuck did not attend the dance last night... there had been other attractions at Duxford. 'Do you think me very wicked, Geoff?' He asked, looking at me with those little daggers of eyes that never stayed still. 'I suppose you're saying to yourself he's an awful swine.' He looked at me apologetically, hoping that I would offer an excuse for him. He was a little worried when I, like a prig, said, 'Yes, I do.'

He thought for a moment and said, 'Well, after all, Geoff, the girl had a good time too and likes it.' 'No,' I said, 'I don't mean with the girl last night but I'm thinking of the other one who hopes you'll marry her.' 'I must tell you of the scene when I woke up this morning,' said Tuck, 'it made me laugh like a drain. I was very

drunk last night and went to bed with the girl from the reception desk. Her name was Miss Marston. The first thing I heard on waking up was a knock on the door and a horrified "Oh, Miss Marston!" from the chambermaid. I was tickled to death and jumped out of bed. That made the chambermaid more confused than ever as I was stark naked.'

Tuck laughed again, hit the table and said, 'Ach, so.' He had a habit of interposing two words of broken German when he was not quite feeling at ease.

During the morning Tuck headed towards France to have 'a thrash round the sky' and 'beat up the other side.' He studied a map of the French coast and headed towards his aircraft.

After walking a few steps he turned back, looked at me and said, 'You know, Geoff, I don't want you to think me sentimental or anything but in case anything should happen, you might give my girl a ring. Here's her telephone number. Cheer ho!'

He dived in and out of the cloud over the French coast, chased a Henschel 126, dived through a gap in the clouds on to St. Omer aerodrome and came back for tea.

Tuck had left the experienced New Zealander, Flying Officer John Martin, to look after any routine convoy patrols. Late in the day, the weather closing in, 257 was ordered to send up two planes on a dusk patrol. When Sergeant Jones, who was due to fly, could not be found, Carl Capon, Tuck's number two pilot, who had already done an hour's flying, volunteered to take his place.

'Come on John,' he said, 'I want to do a bit of dusk-flying. The clouds were low and there were fits of snowstorms... They took off at 5.30pm when it was

almost dark. I felt uneasy. Just after they had taken off, the controller rang me to ask what the weather was like. I said that it was bad, that the cloud base was about 2,000 feet and that it had been snowing. He said, 'Oh.'

At six o'clock the controller and Geoff spoke again, and Myers was assured that they would be back in a few minutes.

I went out onto the aerodrome. A sharp east wind, which had turned the puddles into brittle sheets of ice, was blowing. It seemed a long time before I heard the familiar drone of the Hurricanes. At last I saw the navigation lights of one aircraft circle above the black, open space. I saw the flashes from its recognition light and the aerodrome control pilot flash back his signal to land. Above the red obstruction lights of the hangars the plane circled round again more slowly. I could not stop talking to myself, 'that's it. A little higher … now then … good. A bit of a bump, but quite a good landing.'

As he looked up, Intelligence Officer Myers was surprised to see two more aircraft circling above, although only one other Hurricane had taken off from 257.

I was a bit puzzled but one of the two aircraft circling above must be from the other squadron stationed at Coltishall or from a neighbouring aerodrome. As one of the planes was circling round the field for the last time before landing, a sudden squall of snow blew up.

I could hardly see the green and red dots of light, as the snow blew in my face… chance light on. Jove, how the snow shows up in the chance light beam in a whirling maze of whiteness. Just a glimpse of the navigation lights, then the graceful form of the Hurricane was illuminated by the chance light. Lovely landing.

Myers did not have long to admire the landing as the Hurricane trundled peacefully across the airfield with its white welcome carpet of snow. There was a third plane still to land.

'Good God! What's that? The third aircraft above the middle of the drome at 500 feet. It shouldn't be there. Oh! Stop! No! Oh!'

I bit my lips in agony. The aircraft suddenly appeared to be drunk, reeled to port, banked to starboard. Red, green, white lights whirled around. A gust of snow slapped me in the face. God! The aircraft was going down. There was a great cracking up as it dived nose first into the ground. Not a hope in hell.

Myers shouted for a fire tender and then jumped on the fire engine as it was overtaking him.

The fire tender radiator had a leak and the water was bursting into the driver's face, showing up a shower of golden rain as it was caught in the lights, blinding us all. 'Over there! Over there! To the right,' two or three aircraftsmen yelled at us. We could see nothing. The Hurricane had not caught fire. Its lights were out. As we raced over the field we perceived a mass of wreckage.

'Raiders or no raiders, switch your spot lamp on.' I went up to the wreckage. A gleam of light from the spot lamp illuminated the pilot's head and back, smashed against the ground. 'Who is it?' I tried to recognise the hair, because Martin's hair was golden russet too, like that of Capon.

From the gloves the little group thought that the dead pilot was John Martin, although it was difficult to tell.

The aircraftsmen were looking at the dismal sight, awed by the suddenness, the stillness and the death. 'You'll have to get an axe to hack him out.' As I was

looking at the steaming glycol pouring out of the wreckage, trying to ascertain that nothing would catch fire, Pat suddenly appeared. When he saw the dead body he swayed. 'Come away quickly old boy,' I said as I held him.

Pat had been sleeping off the New Year's party on a sofa in the dispersal room. If he had not been asleep it might have been him out on that routine patrol.

'No, Pat,' I said, 'there's nothing to be done. Go back, old chap. I don't want you to stay here.' 'It's poor old John Martin,' he said, 'they told me that Capon had gone into the dispersal room. Poor old John.'

Just the night before, at the dance in the sergeants' mess on New Year's Eve, John Martin had brought his wife, Edna. They had only married in November, and now he was gone before the end of the first day of the new year.

Poor old John, and there's his wife waiting for him in the ladies' room at the mess, ready for him to take her back to the inn where they're staying. And I'll have to break it to her. She looked lovely, too, in her evening dress at the sergeants' New Year's Eve dance. She and Hugh's wife were the only two girls in evening dress. They were all of a flutter when they found they were not supposed to wear evening dress. Mrs Martin seemed shy and upset... what a long time ago that seemed! And it was last night. How would I tell her? Poor woman.

That would be for later but for now the ground staff needed to get the body of John Martin out of his Hurricane and back into the warmth of the buildings. An aircraftsman said to Myers:

> 'The wreckage is buried very deep, sir, and it's caught him on the legs, so it'll be a bit of a job

to get him out and we'll have to fetch some other tools.' 'All right,' I replied, 'You'd better do that, Sergeant.'

As he turned in the direction of the Mess, knowing that he needed to tell Mrs Martin before she heard the terrible news about her husband from anyone else, he was taken by surprise.

'What?' I thought. 'Good God, have I gone mad?' There, in the beam of the spotlight was John Martin, staggering, glaring... at what? At whom? John Martin? I grabbed hold of him. 'Come away,' I said. 'It's all right, Geoff,' he answered with a sort of groan. 'I'm all right. Don't worry about me. He's dead. It's poor old Capon.'

Yates explained that the third aircraft, from a second squadron based at Coltishall, had been given permission to land first.

I was in turmoil. I took John by the arm, walked slowly across the field with him. He said, 'I was puzzled when I didn't see Capon land. He was coming in after me. I had no idea he had crashed until I saw the spotlight, walked over and then noticed you were there... he must have got caught in the snow squall as he was circling in to land.'

I rushed in in front to tell Pat and warn the others that it was Carl Capon and not John Martin who had been killed.

That night Geoffrey Myers wrote a letter to his young son, Robert.

My little Robert,

Perhaps you will read this one day and ponder over Carl Capon's death. Perhaps you will say, 'But why, oh

why should he, of all the boys, have been killed in this futile way. It seems so unfair.' Don't say that, my little boy. There are things in heaven and earth that we cannot fathom.

Capon was pure and upright. He had no enemies, yet he was active and strong. He had a sense of duty but never gave the impression that he was righteous in carrying it out. When he spoke, he looked at the listener straight in his eyes. If others made foolish mistakes he forgave them, but he was not indulgent for himself. His code of conduct was based upon his conscience. There was no trace of vanity in his make-up and he was always ready to laugh at himself.

My boy, your Dad feels that you will benefit by his example. Perhaps you will gain, through me, inspiration from his death to help you in your pattern of life.

I will not forget Carl Capon. He has helped me, and perhaps he will help you.

A few days later Myers wrote to his family again.

I attended Capon's funeral today... Our train crawled along through an air raid. No lights on. One of us said he saw a bomb drop as we approached London. We arrived at Liverpool Street station just before midnight. We went down the tube. Every corner on the stairs and in the passages crammed with sleepers wrapped in blankets or lying on newspapers spread out on the concrete floors. London tubes are full every night. Air raid wardens, Red Cross nurses and police in steel helmets keep watch. The escalators had stopped running. We walked down and passed by scores more bundles of sleepers. Apart from heavy breathing there was practically no sound.

The tubes had stopped running for the night. We groped our way out of the station to a bus. The city

was still smoking after the great fire caused by the rain of incendiary bombs a few nights previously. Like blind men, lined up on either side of us, gutted business houses, with only their outside structure still standing could be distinguished by the light of the overcast moon. The eyes of the buildings, which used to twinkle with reflected lights from street lamps and passing cars, were now black and hollow. The adjutant shuddered and remarked, 'A city of the dead.'

Perhaps that night the streets would be ablaze with incendiary bombs, and more business houses and churches would crackle and crash under high explosives. I placed my head against the bus window to catch a glimpse of it, because next time I passed by it might be a ruin.

Myers and Freddie Wallis, the adjutant, had been joined at the last minute by the Canadian, Jimmy Cochrane, and Charles Frizzell. They had only been released two days before from many months in hospital and in convalescence, following the drunken car accident the previous year which had also taken Myers himself out of service for three weeks. Both Cochrane and Frizzell had been posted to RAF Debden as non-effective for the next three months.

Jimmy can't see properly out of his left eye and his star turn is to raise his eyebrow alone several times in quick succession. The other brow remains motionless.

We went to the Regent Palace Hotel. The air of first-rate efficiency and second-class luxury was still there, but faces had changed. The reception clerks no longer bowed you in and out of the hall with hasty smiles, but asked you to fill in identity forms with the tired, dry

manner of state officials. 'Take it or leave it' was written on their faces. Enough bombs had fallen in Piccadilly to justify their attitude more than enough.

Nobody seemed to care. Why should hotel guests expect good waiting? Could they not see there were only old men left there? Could guests not realise that meals were being served in and out of air raids night after night? No, they could not. Well, so much for them, and if they complained they would be ignored. The superficial appearance of everything inside the hotel was the same. Drinks were served all night in the lounge, an orchestra accompanied the meals, chambermaids answered bells, the decorations were still garish. But war had crept into the building.

Jimmy Cochrane and Charles Frizzell had booked in at the hotel but had gone out. We met them at the neighbouring Corner House. Jimmy sat down with us and entered into a long monologue of self-accusation. I was struck by the resemblance to the Red Indian which he had painted on his aircraft. Jimmy passed his hand over and over again through his black silky hair and said, 'I've been a shit. I know. Look at the rest of the squadron. I know. Bumped off. And I've been out of it. Honest to God, I didn't want it to happen like this.'

Myers and Wallis tried to reassure him, 'Of course you didn't. Everyone knows that.'

'It's a shit's trick all the same,' he said, 'but I don't feel right yet.' He moved his one eyebrow up and down earnestly to show how fixed the other one was. 'I need a long rest and I want to get back to Canada for a few months before I start again. I want to see my little wifie and my mother.' Jimmy called his young girl his 'wifie'.

Jimmy Cochrane and Wallis stayed up drinking until 4am and the next morning headed to the funeral which was to be held near Capon's house at Surbiton in Surrey.

Jimmy and Charlie looked dismally shabby and dirty when we drove over for the funeral. Charlie had a guilty look about him and apologetically quoted poetry about not breaking faith with the war dead.

There were a few prayers, a commonplace sermon, and a hymn in a bare chapel. An aunt broke down. We bore the coffin to the grave and saluted.

Charles Frizzell thought that Freddie Wallis was still hung-over. 'On the occasion of the funeral, not only did he nearly fall into the grave while attempting a salute, but he introduced me to the bereaved mother as Carl Capon. However, as I recall, all was forgiven at the wake afterwards.'[86]

After the funeral, before they got their train back, the four men went round to Capon's home. Frizzell recalled, 'Carl was very young. I remember going to his funeral, which, for his parents, must have been very sad. This for several reasons – the fact that he was killed by accident must have seemed such a waste.'

We taxied round to Mr Capon's house, had a few drinks with him and talked about the boy who was in all our thoughts. Then we talked vaguely about the war and said goodbye. Mr Capon shook hands warmly with the adj and said, 'Thank you. You're a Briton.' He looked at us earnestly.

On the way back to the station they stopped in a pub. Cochrane and Frizzell, although now out of hospital and convalescence, were not yet back on active service

[86]Letter to Author, March 26 1982

and were certainly not going back to Coltishall to rejoin their squadron.

The adjutant was in a cantankerous world of his own but Jimmy and Charlie did not realise it for a while. 'You boys must come back with us,' the adj insisted, pointing at Jimmy and leering at him. 'You'll be a disgrace to the Air Force if you don't come back with us,' he insisted. 'You bloody little fool. Of course you're a shit. You won't come back with us. You're afraid. You're afraid. You're just a little shit.'

The adjutant poured out a volume of invectives which roused Jimmy to a frenzy, especially as he had also been drinking hard. 'You're just a coward!' yelled the adj. Jimmy hurled his leather gloves in Freddie's face but he took no notice and turned on Charlie. 'You little twerp,' he yelled, 'Why did you join the RAF?'

Finally, the unhappy quartet went their separate ways. Wallis and Myers made it back to Liverpool Street.

After I somehow persuaded the adj to get into the train for Norwich, he sat down and sobbed. Then he fell asleep. When he awoke towards the end of the journey he couldn't remember a thing. He asked me what had happened. 'How awful, Geoff,' he said 'I don't remember that ever happening before. I blacked out completely. I can't remember a thing.'

Myers reflected on the unhappy funeral. Not only had he buried a young pilot he especially liked and respected but he had been a witness to an unpleasant falling-out between colleagues who were basically on the same side. Naturally, this made him more anxious about his family again.

I get sudden terrors when I think about you and the babies. We are fighting for hope, and as long as we are

fighting, hope cannot be destroyed. Oh my Ducky, soon I'll have the courage to take your photo out of my wallet and look at my babies… There is something that binds us together that's so strong that not all the bombs in Europe can smash it.

Chapter Twelve

The relentless silence from his wife in France tormented Geoffrey Myers. Six months had passed now since he had received any news. The last thing he wanted to hear was what he read in the papers. He wrote to his wife that night.

January 17 1941

My Beloved,

I have been struggling all afternoon and evening. Now I feel numbed. Here's the article that did it.

ENGLISHWOMEN AS TARGETS FOR THE RAF (Daily Mail, January 14 1941):

British women of all ages, rounded up by the Germans from occupied France, are being sent to concentration camps near military objectives which are frequent targets of the RAF. Sites for some of these camps have been specially chosen near bases such as Lorient. The detention at first only applied to men of military age and young boys and older men who were mere prisoners on parole. But in December the measure was generalised and boys of fourteen years and men of sixty-five and over were taken first to prison and then to concentration camps. On December 5 the measure was made applicable to women, including those of French birth who were married to Englishmen.

In most cases only one hour's warning was given, and the women, young and old – I have heard of one case of a woman of eighty-eight being interned – were taken away with only 30lbs of luggage. In Normandy, for instance, eight British women were taken to the gaol of the country town and kept there for two days. An informant, who has visited these camps, expressed his admiration at their wonderful spirit and absolute confidence in their country. But he added the urgent appeal that an American or other neutral committee be formed to supply these camps whenever possible with extra comforts and to obtain the right for these women to correspond with their families.

Luckily, Margot Myers and her family had not been rounded up and were still hiding at Beaurepaire. They were safe but deeply anxious. The pressure on Jews in France was growing all the time. News reached Margot that three Jews had been arrested in the nearby town of Moulins which was at the border, the demarcation line, between the large part of France occupied by the Nazis and collaborationist Free France led by Marshal Pétain.

To her horror, Margot discovered that one of her aunts was a supporter of Pétain. Even in her own family there was danger and so she kept her half-Jewish children well away from the aunt. She knew that even with the risks in so-called Free France, she had no choice but to cross the border and try to escape before the Nazis knocked on the farmhouse door.

With no news from his wife for so many long months, the article in the *Daily Mail* had deeply unsettled Myers.

Up till today I was sure you were at Beaurepaire. I don't know what's happening. Is it true or is it a nightmare that a journalist has created without caring?

I've telephoned friends and written to the Red Cross and Foreign Office to try to find out the truth. For weeks I have been trying to train myself to be cheerful and calm. Now this. Men can keep up their spirits with their limbs shot away. This sort of torture is different.

The snow on the ground, which had begun to thaw, has frozen and formed rivers of ice along all the paths of the camp. The wind cuts through one's clothes and the officers shiver in their great coats. I've read that the temperature is much colder in France.

When you were cold, my love, I used to warm you. I have central heating in my room and three warm blankets. Oh my Lovvie, how it all hurts. I can't help thinking of the cold, of the separation from the babies, of your tears. My God, what have I brought upon you through our marriage?

Geoffrey did everything he could to find out if the details outlined in the article were based on fact.

I have been through nights of torture. I have had difficulty in controlling my body which kept trembling like a leaf on an oak tree in winter. I have been through convulsions, searching my mind to know what to do. It all happened at the same time. I wrote to the Red Cross and the Foreign Office asking for any information they could give me about the women interned in France. I kept on saying to myself that the *Daily Mail* article was a lie, but could not understand how it got past the censorship and so thought there might be something in it. My friend, whom I phoned the day I read the article, was unable to find out anything. I scanned every newspaper. Then I read this:

REPRISALS ACTION IN FRANCE (Sunday Dispatch, January 19 1941)

Berlin disclosed yesterday that about 3,000 British subjects, many of them women, have been rounded up in occupied France and placed in internment camps. The camps are situated amongst other places at Besançon and Le Bourget. At Besançon there are men, women and children.

Diplomatic sources say they did not know the total number of British subjects interned in occupied France. The Germans said the reason for this latest round-up was 'military necessity'. It was understood, however, that it was in part a reprisal for the internment of Germans in various parts of the British empire.

It was partial confirmation of the article. I continued to read every newspaper in the mess and arranged to go to London for a few days' leave in the hope of finding out more.

Although her husband, naturally fearing the worst, didn't know it, Margot Myers and their children were still safely hidden at the family home in central France, 'I could feel the net closing in on us little by little,' she recalled later.[87] The Germans were all over Lucenay-lès-Aix and the surrounding area, making Margot afraid. She feared bring locked up in the notorious Mal Coiffée prison in Moulins before being shipped off to a concentration camp. She had already hidden the children's British passports and destroyed all signs of any Jewish background. With her mother, she now worked the land even harder so that there was enough food to feed the family without having to travel into nearby villages to buy supplies.

[87]Margot Myers memoir, translated by her daughter, Anne

One day, Margot felt that the German noose had finally closed round her family's neck. She saw in the distance a German soldier on a motorbike making his way up towards the house. Was he looking for Jews? Or English children? Margot's heart pounded. Even her little son Robert could sense the tension amongst the adults and then the relief as the soldier smiled and asked in halting French if he could purchase some eggs.

Myers was acutely aware during this time that he had a responsibility to his squadron as well as his stranded family.

I'm going to try and talk to you tonight about us all over here and keep my thoughts from wandering away to you. I haven't been able to write to you because I haven't been calm enough. I think I have kept cheerful among the pilots. I haven't moped in a corner, but have joked with them as usual, and they have been at ease with me.

Geoff describes to his wife the squadron's dance at the Lido in mid-January. In particular, he was interested to meet Cowboy Blatchford's girlfriend, Betty.

When the hall had filled up I noticed them both, running downstairs and then sailing off together on the dance floor, rather like a dinghy caught in a squall. She was plump and stocky, like him. She probably had light-brown hair but it was now bleached, golden and rather patchy. I was struck by the resemblance of their eyes. Hers, too, was a determined face. 'I like you, Geoff, because you're Peter's friend,' she said, 'and I adore Peter.'

We went into the bar and she tossed off two or three gin and limes, like a man. She pretended to be proud of the quantity she could drink, and bragged about

being able to swallow a pint of beer in ten seconds. I began to understand things when somebody told me she could sail a yacht on the Broads as well as any man in Norfolk.

Bob Stanford Tuck was there with his girlfriend and was determined that his entire squadron have a great time. Myers kept an eye on proceedings, supporting and encouraging as usual. One young pilot looked on jealously as a senior Polish flyer danced gaily with the man's wife.

'I'm glad you find her pretty in that dress, Geoff. She made it herself. I find she looks pretty too, Geoff.' Hugh never felt quite sure of himself. He was only twenty and had not yet brought down an enemy plane, for all his keenness. He felt he was clumsy and that he did silly things.

His wife, pretty, small and gay, thought it just as well that he continued to feel like that. 'I'm glad you like her, Geoff,' he said, and looked at me for approval.' 'I do old boy, I think she's charming.' Hugh smiled with satisfaction. He liked to hear that from a married man who loved his own wife.

The crowd yelled for more music. The bar, which was open until midnight because it had been transformed into a 'club', was crowded with airmen eager to enjoy this privilege [to the full].

The local police chief, transformed into a dance master for the night, acted as referee in the waltz competition. The girls from Smith's spice factory were now warm and jolly. 'The Blue Danube' which the Nazis had first chased out of Austria and then from the whole continent still swayed the dancers here. Everyone was in high spirits.

Myers was a friend but also a great admirer of Peter Blatchford. He knew that he always had the interests of his men at heart. When the sector controller tried to get 257 to fly in the wintry dusk about a week later, Blatchford was having none of it. Many of the squadron still remembered Carl Capon's futile death in a snowstorm a few weeks earlier.

Blatchford went to the telephone with a big frown clouding his face. He grabbed the mouthpiece and started hammering out a few short sentences. 'I flatly refuse to allow any of my chaps to go up after dark,' he said, and laid his fist down on the desk. 'I don't want to be unpleasant with you, sir, but we have this fight every night.' 'I didn't mean to be rude to him. Geoff,' he said, 'but I got so bloody angry.'

Cowboy Blatchford and Myers were two of the men in 257 most respected and liked by David Hunt and his wife, Terry. They clearly cared about David and were concerned for his progress. David had been transferred from Billericay to the Centre for Plastic and Jaw Surgery at Queen Victoria Hospital in East Grinstead – the pioneering Burns Unit run by the legendary surgeon McIndoe. Here, badly burned patients were often treated with experimental techniques – and as a result, David and his fellow patients became members of the famous Guinea Pig Club.

Happily, the plastic surgery worked and David could finally see again. Terry wrote, *'There he was with heavy eyelids, red and gold… after a time he reached for the mirror and looked at himself for a long time. I asked him if he was pleased, and he supposed he would have to be. In any case, he was pleased to see again, even if things did quiver a bit and he had to hold open his eyes with his fingers because the lids felt so heavy. He found the* Daily Mirror *and began to read.'*

Despite the endless operations, the wards in East Grinstead were probably much livelier than 257's base near Norwich. Coltishall was stiff and dull for the young pilots, so they did their best to create some fun. The social calendar continued with a cocktail party to brighten up the morgue-like atmosphere. Peter Blatchford decided to bring his girlfriend, Betty, to the party.

Peter did not mention his 'girlfriend' for some time. He tackled me the evening before the cocktail party.

Blatchford leant against the sideboard, frowning. Then he cleared the wrinkles away with a sweep of his hand, raised his eyebrows and looked me straight in the eye. 'My girlfriend's coming to the cocktail party tomorrow night, Geoff... I feel she's going to speak to you. She knows that you're my friend and that I listen to you... tell her what you think, Geoff. I met her at the pub and we somehow hit it off. I didn't think it mattered at the time. Some days later she told me she was married. I didn't know she was married until something had bound us together. I feel it's wrong, Geoff. If I go on there'll be a disaster. You must help me out of this, Geoff.'

Clearly, Blatchford trusted Myers saying, **'there's something deep within you that you can never kid.'**

I was flustered and a bit perplexed. 'What's the husband like?' I asked. Blatchford shook his head. 'That's the trouble. He's all right. She says she's very fond of him and says he's a fine chap. He's joined up and is somewhere in the north of England. If he were a shit

I wouldn't mind but now I'm the shit. You must talk to her, Geoff.'

Everyone was in party spirits. There was copious amounts of alcohol and the dreary mess had been decorated with palms. It didn't take long for Blatchford's girlfriend, Betty, to single Myers out in the crowded anteroom. Myers was embarrassed and unsure what to say. He thought that it was nothing to do with him.

'Oh yes it is,' said Betty,' you're his best friend and you influence him. I must tell you all about it.' I hurried out of the crowded room. Betty followed me quickly and tucked her arm under mine. We walked along the passage into the ladies' room which had been set up as a cocktail bar and was to be opened in an hour's time. It was empty. What a relief!

Betty sat on the bar. In her habitual direct manner she charged in again. 'I'm a Catholic. I don't know if you knew that. I was an idealist. Now I'm the other thing. You know what I mean? The opposite to idealist, what's it called? Oh, yes, fatalist. I'm a fatalist now.

'I loved my husband and I wanted children badly. They did not come at first. I waited ... I waited,' she continued and looked up at me pathetic and appealing. 'At last I had two lovely twin boys. They were...'

The conversation was interrupted by two young pilots looking for bottles of alcohol.

When they had shut the door, Betty, who was almost in tears, grabbed hold of both my arms for support and, taking no notice of the interruption, continued. 'Those lovely little babies of mine both died a few days after they were born. There was no reason to do that. God wouldn't have done that. It broke something in me.'

Betty's story was interrupted yet again. This time it was the genial mess secretary who had popped into the room for a drink. Quite unaware of the emotion that was swirling through the room he insisted that Betty and Geoff join him in a sherry. As soon as he could, Myers escaped to the ping-pong room which had been converted into the cloakroom for the evening.

Betty picked up the bits of her appeal and said, 'How can I feel the same as before, Geoff? It wasn't fair. I was longing for those little boys.'

'You have been through a terrible time,' I blurted out, 'I can understand what a gap it must have made in your life.'

'I have a friend who had three miscarriages… but mine were alive, Geoff. Now this has happened with Cowboy… that's why I have become a fatalist.'

'It's not for me to approve or not approve. All I care is that Cowboy can go on with his work and hold his head high. The trouble is that he is miserable over all this, utterly miserable, and I believe you are too.'

'No I'm not, Geoff,' she said, 'I'm dreadfully happy and so is Cowboy.'

That evening Freddy Wallis, the adjutant, was in a state.

The dance music was jerking out and the couples moved swiftly round. Freddy saw me and said, 'It's awful, I have only had two or three whiskies tonight and I'm not tiddly, but I know something dreadful is happening outside my room. There are spies in this place, Geoff. I know I heard German just outside my door.'

Myers suggested the possibility that it might have been batmen, several of whom were Irish, talking in Gaelic.

Freddy was immensely relieved. Two Irishmen had been on duty in his wing last night and had been having a chat in Irish. He was as pleased as a child who gets into a nice warm bed after a frightening run in the dark.

A few days later, Myers wrote in his notebooks about Betty once again.

My Darlings,

Peter Blatchford has been going to Norwich of an evening and returning the next morning early. He has been looking more and more glum and has been drinking heavily. He has not exactly been avoiding me, but things have been different. We have not been able to look each other in the face quite so clearly. When we were alone together I said to him, 'You made a bloody fool of me the other day, Peter. I ought to have known better. In the ordinary way I would have kept well out of that business with Betty, but as you appealed to me to say what I thought I did so. After thinking it over I can't help feeling that the whole thing was a bit absurd. I don't suppose you meant to make a fool of me but it looks as if it was a bit of a frame-up on Betty's part.'

After that I talked of something else.

Chapter Thirteen

In France, Margot and her children survived the winter. At one point the electricity was cut off for a fortnight. On her trips into a local town or village she noticed an increase in German propaganda and a resulting rise in anti-British feeling. Newspapers had turned against Jews. Her cousin, like her aunt, now identified as a Pétainist.

Her Uncle Guy visited Beaurepaire and had been full of stories of Jews – even children – being rounded up in Paris. 'That's when I made up my mind I was going to leave.'[88] Margot realised she had to escape, somehow. Her mother tried briefly to deter her, saying that the children would be safe where they were and that it would be more dangerous to try to escape. But Margot begged her mother not to hinder her. She knew that she needed every ounce of courage and confidence to carry her escape plan through. Her mother said no more.

One day in January, 1941, Margot received a surprising but rather non-committal letter sent via Portugal from her mother-in-law in England. She wondered at the blandness of the anodyne letter, until she understood. The letter was not from her mother-in-law at all but from Geoffrey. At the beginning of the war they had

[88]Memoirs of Margot Myers translated by her daughter, Anne

agreed a simple code between them but this was the first message she had received from England for more than six months, and she had never used the code before. She tried to remember what it was and then she finally recalled it. A German codebreaker would not have found it troublesome. Later her son Robert worked it out. The date at the top of the letter referred to words, so a letter sent on the fourth day of the month meant the message was to be understood by connecting every fourth word. Margot fell upon the letter with glee. The message from her husband was simple. It said, 'Get out. Go to Lisbon.'

At the same time, Geoff was desperately trying to find out more about what was really happening to British women in France. He took a couple of days' leave to go down to London from Coltishall.

On the eve of my trip to London I read the following in *The Times*:

British subjects in Paris. About 3,000 interned at Besançon.

Myers also noted a statement from the Foreign Secretary, Anthony Eden, in a written reply to a question about British arrests in France. The statement said:

On December 5 and the following five days a large number of British women of all ages and men over the age of sixty-five were arrested by the German authorities in Paris and were sent to the Caserne Vauban at Besançon, France, for internment. During the process of arrest and internment the United States Embassy in Paris kept in touch with the German authorities by personal visits and by telephone and did everything possible to relieve the hardships involved in this sudden and widespread measure of internment.

Doctors, German Red Cross nurses and special food for mothers and children were dispatched by the German authorities and, although sleeping facilities for the first few days were not sufficient, by December 15 everything had been organised and each internee had a bed. In addition to the German Red Cross nurses there is a large number of English nurses and nursing nuns among the internees. The Caserne is heated and health conditions are good. Mothers with children under sixteen and women over sixty are to be released, unless there are special reasons for the detention. Released internees will not be allowed to return to their homes, but will be required to select new residences in the eastern part of France.

There are approximately 3,000 men, women and children at Caserne Vauban. 685 men who had hitherto not been interned at Saint-Denis have now been interned at Drancy.

Drancy, in north-eastern Paris, was soon to become the notorious internment camp where thousands of Jews were incarcerated, before being shipped off to concentration camps like Auschwitz. During the war more than 67,000 Jews were deported from Drancy to extermination camps.

For Myers, the speech from Anthony Eden outlining the likelihood of release for women and young children, was of comfort.

I am greatly relieved, because at least I felt that you were not suffering from hunger and cold, and that there was a good chance of your release.

So Myers headed for London, caught somewhere between anxiety and relief, determined to find out more.

A kind lady at the British Red Cross Society told me all she knew about conditions in France, but could add nothing to the Foreign Secretary's statement. She said she would let me know as soon as lists were received of the names of the internees. She took out a little notebook marked 'Promises' and wrote my name down in it.

I knew the poor, tired woman had probably repeated the same thing to hundreds of anxious inquirers and had reassured them to the best of her ability. I was moved by her goodness and tried to slip ten shillings in the collection box, then felt foolish because it wouldn't go through the hole which was meant only for coins. She helped it down with a smile.

Myers continued his inquiries by visiting the Foreign Office.

The official, a pleasant ex-serviceman from the last war, showed me the boundaries of the territory in which the British women who were released would be allowed to live. 'It looks as if it may just include Moulins,' he said, 'and they may not have interned with your wife at all. Of course, you never know. They may have arrested her out of sheer cussedness and would then move her. We don't know the position yet, but we are waiting for names from the American Embassy.'

Geoff then went to see his friend, John, whose name he had given his wife as a possible point of contact. At John's flat in Lancaster Gate there was good news waiting for Myers. Two telegrams had arrived earlier that day, sent on a circuitous route via a friend in Clermont-Ferrand. Margot had finally managed to smuggle out messages to the man in Clermont for onward delivery to her husband in the UK.

From these telegrams I knew that you were still at Beaurepaire [as recently as] December, as it said that a letter had been sent to me then. I knew that conditions were excellent on the farm then, and that you are well. You asked whether I still advised you to return. I was keyed up with excitement and hope.

It was the first news I had received since September 10 and it came at a moment when I was most anxious about you all. I could not tell, however, how long it has taken you to get the message through to unoccupied France. All I know was that you had written, or got our friends in Clermont-Ferrand to write to me, some time in December. I knew that the arrests had taken place between December 5 and 15. I could not tell if you had been interned after the message had been passed through. My impression was that you were still free.

Myers discussed the reply with his friend, John.

Good-hearted John was as excited over the telegrams as I. He screwed his eyes up in delight and laughed. 'You needn't worry about what Margot will do at her end. I know how sensible she is,' he said. 'If you've any fear about that end, all I can say is that I know your wife better than you do.'

The men reasoned that if the question was 'Do you advise getting out?' it meant that Margot had worked out a way of crossing from occupied France into the unoccupied or free zone to the south.

I thought it over... You would know how to cross the border into unoccupied territory without undue risk. If you were still free the Germans would be bound to find out sooner or later that you were the wife of an Englishman and they would then discover that you were the wife of a Jew and a journalist, the combination of all

that is hated by the Nazis. They would have grounds for arresting you, saying that you concealed your identity. You would be taken away from the babies, as I feared all along. The course was obvious.

An hour later I wired, 'Advise immediate return.' I felt happy about this and slept well.

Myers had talked to his journalist friends in Europe and worked out that the safest route to the UK was to cross the demarcation line into the unoccupied zone and then to travel by train down through France, probably to Toulouse. Then, by train again, to Barcelona and Madrid. From Spain it should be reasonably straightforward to get into neutral Portugal where he knew that seats on a plane or ship to the UK might be available.

It looked simple on paper but he knew that it wasn't. He had enormous faith in the courage and good sense of his wife. However, she had two young children to look after and having a Jewish husband who was also in the RAF put the family at permanent risk. It could go wrong at any time, from the first day trying to secretly cross the demarcation line, to the final leg of the journey from Lisbon, especially if that had to go by ship.

Myers also overestimated how easy it would be for Margot and her two young children to slip across the demarcation line without being arrested. Knowledge of how to achieve this was not widely accessible because secrecy was paramount to the resistance efforts.

Margot Myers also realised that she could not evade the Nazis for long. A poster was put up in the local village. It said, 'People who know anyone who is English should denounce them.' When Margot was anxiously reading this, a neighbour shouted to her in a loud voice,

'What are you going to do about it?'[89] Fortunately, no one heard, but it was time to move on.

Early in 1941, Margot Myers, by now fully determined to escape, noticed that the grocer's son in the local village of Lucenay had disappeared. The grocer, Monsieur Duguet, had an unofficial reputation as an expert in smuggling people across the demarcation line. Margot knew that the grocer's boy hadn't been picked up by the Germans, so she presumed that he was in danger in another way and had needed to escape. Perhaps he was an active member of the resistance? Or perhaps he had just crossed the border to resume his studies as a clockmaker? She did not know and did not ask.

At a quiet moment, when there were no other customers in his shop, she approached the grocer herself. Monsieur Duguet had qualms even though he had known Margot's family for many years. His wife made the decision for him as Margot revealed, '[She] was very nice and also intelligent and energetic. When I told her about my plans, and while her husband was hesitating, she took things in hand.'[90] They said it would be very tricky but that he would try to arrange it.

For some months there had been a number of ways to illegally cross the demarcation line at Moulins – by foot, by boat, even hidden in barrels or carts of manure. Some smugglers took these risks for money; others, like the grocer who helped the Myers family, as acts of defiance or resistance.

In Moulins itself, in 1941, the dungeons at La Mal Coiffée had become an official German military prison

[89]Margot Myers, interview with Janet Willis
[90]Memoirs of Margot Myers translated by her daughter, Anne

with Jews and resistance fighters the main inmates. Margot timed her escape well. Maybe she sensed that the German military prison was quickly becoming a stronghold of the Gestapo and a place of physical persecution. 'The instruments of torture at the Mal Coiffée are very simple: they are the revolver butt, the tongs, the nerve, the wire, the bathtub and, above all, the hunger, the thirst, moral torture… The Germans take revenge by manual correction… punches that hurt, assault, sometimes kill.'[91]

In London, Myers was feeling less confident following another visit to the Foreign Office, the day after he had sent his message to Margot in France advising her to escape. He told the official what he had decided.

The official was dubious. 'Of course,' he said, 'a number of people have been smuggled across the border at Moulins but I don't see how your wife will be able to manage with two babies. The difficulties are very great. She might dress up as a peasant woman and amble across the fields or get into a hay cart. The people down there know the ways.'

I was starting to get anxious. 'Do you know if many people get caught crossing the border?' I asked. 'Well,' he said, smiling uneasily, 'we only hear of the people that get across. We don't know what happens to the others.'

'Do you think my advice was bad?' I asked, feeling thoroughly scared by then. 'No,' he replied. 'As it is she may find the task of crossing the border too difficult

[91]Jacky Tronel blog: Prison History and Military Justice. He is quoting a former prisoner, Yvonne Henri Monceau in her 1945 memoir *Une Prison militaire allemande, à Moulins: La Mal-Coiffée*

and will probably stay where she is, if she has not been interned. In that case, she will have tried.'

Geoff was now in a high state of anxiety. The attempt at reassurance by the official, a kindly man, sounded hollow.

The only thing that stuck in his mind was that a Foreign Office official considered the crossing of the border a very difficult matter. **It confirmed what I had originally thought. My mind was in turmoil.**

Clearly his plan to prepare his family's escape to England via Portugal, by obtaining visas from the American authorities, was not possible. There was no way that he could acquire visas so far in advance and, if he acted too hastily or openly now, there was a risk of compromising their safety further.

'I am afraid that you will have to wait until they get across into unoccupied territory,' the official said kindly, 'because if you did anything now, you would compromise the Americans who are helping us, and also your wife. I think you will have to wait to hear from her before doing anything.'

What had I done? Perhaps I had advised you to move away from a safe place into danger and you would get caught crossing the border.

'The trouble is,' I said, 'she will probably not be able to bring her British passport with her and she may find herself in occupied France without any papers.' After thinking things over the official replied, 'We can let the American authorities know and ask them to issue her with a temporary passport. That will be all right.'

Geoff had an American friend, John Elliott, a journalist on the *New York Herald Tribune* who was based in Vichy, where Pétain's government had their headquarters. Vichy was also not too far from the border with occupied France. Myers debated with himself and his friend in London whether to contact his Elliott or not. He did not want to compromise his American friend, nor his friends in Clermont-Ferrand, if he used them as a conduit for a message again. For the moment he did nothing.

The more I thought about it, the greater the danger of crossing the border seemed to grow. I had pictures of you and the children being stopped by German sentries. And then, suppose you did get across, it was a toss-up as to whether unoccupied France would stay free for long. You might get caught while trying to obtain visas for England. And if you did reach England you might arrive just before an invasion and I would have nowhere for you to go. I might have been killed, and then you would have left home to feel isolated in our beleaguered island.

Your second telegram made me think you were in Beaurepaire. Perhaps I have done the wrong thing. Something inside me kept repeating, 'He who hesitates is lost.' But I could not help revolving over and over again in my mind the picture of your being caught at the border of being overtaken by an invasion of unoccupied France.

The newspapers were reporting that the Nazis were threatening to occupy the whole of France. Time was short for the escape plan to succeed. Geoffrey and his friend debated through all the different options for hours but, in the end, concluded that the correct decision had been made.

In France, Margot Myers was already confirming her plans to leave. She arranged another discreet meeting with the grocer and his wife. Monsieur Duguet said that although it was difficult he was working on a plan. His wife told Margot that they would introduce her to a gamekeeper and his wife from nearby Dompierre. He was responsible for land on both sides of the demarcation line.

'Thanks to their grocery business the Duguets had a small petrol allowance and went once a week to Dompierre to replenish their stocks. So one day they took me along to meet the gamekeeper and his wife. I explained the situation and things were soon settled. There had been no mention of money.'[92]

A few days later the Myers received a message from the grocer and his wife to meet on a certain date, 'Don't bring any luggage,' they had told me, 'bring only your passports and indispensable papers. My wife will take you on the road and I'll slip through the woods with the papers. Dress as though you are going from one farm to the other. You must especially look as if you are not going off on a trip. The family should just appear normal, no luggage, no special clothes; they just needed to look as if they were going for a walk, and to have passports and other essential papers.'

Finally, the day came to escape, 'Leaving Beaurepaire was terrible. We said goodbye to my mother and grandmother. Aunt Marcelle accompanied us on her bike. I was pedalling too, with the two kids behind in the trailer. When we reached the rise before La Chapelle, Aunt Marcelle stopped. We said goodbye, and, weeping, she watched us continue on our way.'[93]

[92]Memoirs of Margot Myers translated by her daughter, Anne
[93]Memoirs of Margot Myers translated by her daughter, Anne

Robert, who was only four years old at the time, recalled, 'At Beaurepaire everybody was weeping. It was difficult to leave. I remember Beaurepaire gradually receding as I looked back from the trailer behind my mother's bicycle.'[94]

At that moment, as her aunt cycled back towards the family home, Margot had no idea when, or if, she would ever see her mother, grandmother and aunt again. England, and her husband, seemed impossibly distant. She was caught between wanting to be with her French family and needing to be safe with her husband once again. Now, she was responsible for two young children, with thousands of miles of danger ahead.

After a few miles of hard cycling, Margot and her two small children arrived at the grocer's. Leaving the bicycle behind they climbed into his van and were driven south to Dompierre. There, he introduced them again to the gamekeeper responsible for the cross-border forest. The safest way across the demarcation line was through that forest, but if they were to be caught it would be obvious that the gamekeeper had arranged their escape and they could not compromise his safety.

The only other option was to smuggle themselves over at a quiet remote crossing. 'The gamekeeper and his wife greeted us kindly. We ate lunch with them. I gave them a good amount of cash in an envelope. They accepted, but told us that was not why they were helping me. I told them I knew it and thanked them warmly.'[95]

The family said a grateful goodbye to the grocer and handed the gamekeeper their precious passports which

[94]Interview with Author 2020

[95]Memoirs of Margot Myers translated by her daughter, Anne

he hid under his belt. In return, Margot was given the identity card of an acquaintance of the gamekeeper who lived in the free zone. Margot was to assume the identity of the other woman, Marie-Louise, should the Myers family be stopped and questioned by the Nazis on guard – and meanwhile, the gamekeeper would meet the family on the other side of the demarcation line.

Margot took one look at the identity card and prayed she would not be stopped. The card did not even have a photograph and, if questioned, Margot was instructed to say it had peeled off. No one would believe this story for a second, she thought, but was determined to carry on.

In 1941 the border at the demarcation line was marked by a large notice, headed *Avis aux Juifs*, 'Notice to Jews'. 'It is forbidden for Jews to cross the demarcation line to visit the occupied zone of France. Jews are those who belong to the Jewish religion. Any Infringement of this Order shall be punished by imprisonment or fine.'

Margot took charge of two-year-old Anne in her pushchair, while the gamekeeper's wife pushed Robert on his bicycle. They walked for several kilometres along the crossing, much of it on a muddy footpath where they met no one else.

One of Robert's earliest memories, aged nearly five, was how cold and wet they were. 'I still remember that the rain was so hard it seemed to be bouncing upwards. I asked the gamekeeper's wife about it. She said it meant that the rain would stop soon. I didn't understand how dangerous it was but somehow I understood that we had to behave.'[96]

[96]Interview with Robert Myers, February 2020

The Moulin de la Cropte, very close to the demarcation line itself, was a well-known staging post for one of the *passeurs,* or smugglers, who specialised in slipping escapers across the line. Robert Myers thinks it is possible that the family sheltered at the Moulin for a time.

The rain thundered down, soaking the small band of escapees to the skin. Luckily the border guards were so focused on staying dry they missed the woman with her two half-English children as they slipped quietly across, very wet but safe.

Margot did not know then just how remarkably fortunate she and her children had been. A Jewish woman, Julie Abid, was arrested a year later as she tried to cross the demarcation line at Moulins with her daughter, Germaine. They were imprisoned at La Mal Coiffée before being transported to Drancy and then onto Auschwitz. The woman who may have sheltered them at the Moulins de la Cropte, Catherine Gouby, a member of the resistance at Dompierre, was also arrested in 1942 and was incarcerated in the dungeons at La Mal Coiffée. Later in the war she was sent to the camp at Ravensbrück.[97]

In fact, Margot had got even closer to capture than she knew. A few days after the family had secretly crossed the demarcation line, the Germans came to her village and demanded that the mayor tell them where an Englishwoman called Mrs Myers lived. Margot had escaped just in time, but the dangers were not over yet.

The family were wet and rain-sodden following their border-crossing, so they sheltered in a cafe in a small

[97]Amis de la Fondation pour la memoire de la Deportation de l'Allier

village just across the border. The owner, however, who was fed up with refugees, threw them back out into the rain. At that moment, fortunately, the gamekeeper arrived, having made his way across the border through the forest. He swapped the French identity card back for Margot's passport. Then he found a car that would take the family on to Vichy. But Margot instinctively did not trust the driver who she thought was 'an adventurer'.[98] She did not feel safe with him and was concerned that he might inform on her by telling the authorities of the family's whereabouts.

She remembered, 'The gamekeeper said to the driver, threateningly, "if anything happens to these children you'll have to answer to me," but I was still worried that the driver would sell us out, denounce us, inform Vichy.'

The man stopped the car in Lapalisse to run some errands and Margot used this as an excuse to get out of the car too. She told him that she did not want to go on because the children were tired. The man looked surprised but shrugged and left. Margot was relieved that he had gone and she felt safer now. Although Anne had slept some of the way, the children were exhausted. She was too.

They found a local hotel. Margot was fearful that the hotelier would be as hostile as the cafe-owner in the last village but the opposite was the case. No questions were asked. They had brought no luggage or spare clothes so Margot stripped the children and put them straight to bed. The woman who ran the hotel kindly offered to dry off their soaking clothes in front of the dining room stove, before the arrival of her customers.

[98]Interview with Janet Willis

The next morning, the hotel helped her find a lift further into the unoccupied zone, to the house of an old friend. A young employee of the local garage drove them for a large sum of money.

Some weeks before, Margot had received a message from an old school friend who lived on the unoccupied side – just – of the border at La Busserie. The message from her friend simply said 'come here if you are in need.' Margot knocked on their door. Her friends were astonished but embraced the family, 'They welcomed us with open arms and unforgettable warmth. All this affected the young man who had brought us there. Again and again he repeated, "You're going to be happy now, won't you?"'[99] For the time being, at least, Margot felt her family were safe.

In Britain, her husband knew none of this. For the rest of his short leave, he decided to visit his mother in the relatively peaceful surroundings of the Oxfordshire countryside. He needed to clear his head and think.

In the train I went on composing telegrams. I wondered how you would cross the border. Would it be at night, after word had passed round that the roads were clear? Perhaps it would be with our friend, Georges Renard, in Clermont-Ferrand, who worked for Michelin and perhaps had retained his car for that reason. Perhaps, again, you might obtain papers under a false name or even under your own name, as a Frenchwoman. But supposing you were stopped?

Dull, flat countryside with factories in every other field on either side of the railway line… a bomb crater here

[99]Memoirs of Margot Myers translated by her daughter, Anne

and there, and some shattered windows. Surprisingly little damage as a whole.

Perhaps you would travel by train. Robert would be good. He would understand. Anne was too young. She might be difficult, the little darling. Supposing you were caught?

He decided to send another telegram after all. This time to his friends in Clermont-Ferrand suggesting that they get in touch with his American journalist contact, John Elliott, in Vichy. He reasoned that if his first telegram, which urged immediate return, was deemed too dangerous by the people in Clermont-Ferrand, then they would hold on to it, rather than try to smuggle it to Margot in the occupied zone.

When I passed the telegram through, I felt better but not reassured. I waded in gumboots through the yard to a black cottage and found Mother. I could not conceal my troubled state, so I told her what had happened. Poor Mother had enough worries already... Were you still at the farm or had you been taken away before receiving my message? Would you get through? Should I not have sent a message hinting at caution? Should I send another telegram? Something again said inside me, 'He who hesitates is lost.'

In Oxfordshire, Myers visited the cottage he had imagined living in one day with his family, if they were ever reunited. Now it was a damp wreck.

This is the home I thought would be so lovely for our little family. The rain came through the roof... everything was damp. The paper was peeling off the walls in the sitting room. The cows had got through the hedge and had eaten the cauliflowers.

Where were you? My calmness had gone, I would have to pull myself together. Perhaps you were interned because you married me? When we married it seemed right to us.

I could not write to you in the evenings. I was too perturbed and realised I would have to wait. I was glad to go back to the squadron and find plenty of work to do. I am with the boys again now.

Chapter Fourteen

On January 26 1941, Bob Stanford Tuck and Peter Blatchford flew over to RAF Bircham Newton near King's Lynn to attend an investiture by King George VI, then at Sandringham. Tuck received the DSO and a bar to the DFC. The citation read, 'This officer has commanded his squadron with great success, and his outstanding leadership, courage and skill has been reflected in its high morale and efficiency…'

But this was just a brief respite from the continuing struggles of the war.

My darlings,

Sergeant Barnes has been promoted to Pilot Officer. He has come over into the officers' mess and is now trying hard to stop calling the other officers 'sir'. Today, he and another pilot, a Czech from Prague [Sergeant Vaclav Brejcha], shot down a Dornier 17 bomber into the sea. It had just dropped bombs in the main street of Lowestoft, killing fourteen persons, and was making for Holland. After they had made three attacks each the bomber, which had come down from 3,000 feet to sea level, dove into the water. One of the Germans jumped when the plane was 150 feet above the sea. He disappeared and so did the bottom rear gunner. The top rear gunner's body was found floating in the water. He had received a number of bullets through his head. The

pilot was saved. He said that he had dropped no bombs. He said the right thing.

It is satisfactory to write combat reports about victories which are clear-cut and in which we have no losses. The thing can be treated as a sporting game, but you mustn't forget that the score is in points of death. If you start thinking about that, you feel the gloom floating heavily about a German pilots' mess, just the other side of the Channel. A good comrade, a good fighter, who won't return for the promised night out in Amiens or Abbeville. Perhaps he was a decent man who brought back comforts to the French family on whom he was billeted. He was probably brave. Most German pilots are brave, like our own.

Not that such an empathetic view of enemy pilots was common. When Myers enquired if the rescue launch had been sent to search for the Germans who had crashed into the sea off Corton, near Lowestoft, he was berated by the operations officer.

'Why did you bother to ring up to find out if we had sent a launch to those buggers who crashed in the sea this afternoon, Geoff?' one of my operations officers asked me. 'Because there was a chance they were alive,' I said. 'We would have been better off letting them all drown,' he replied. The operations officer looked at me angrily. 'If you think they deserve any consideration after killing civilians in the streets of Lowestoft, dropping bombs in the middle of the town, you've got a funny idea of war.'

I thought of our pilots being sent to attack Channel Ports. They too dropped bombs on coastal towns. Sometimes they did not get back, probably shot down somewhere over the sea. Leave the buggers to drown? A slow struggle against the tide. Icy waters gradually

numbing the fingers, then the limbs. General numbness and death.

'Perhaps I have,' I said, 'but I'm glad to say it's shared by the authorities who have ordered the rescue of German pilots from the sea wherever possible.'

Some people have never thought about what we are fighting for… The will to fight in Britain existed among men who cherished freedom and were willing to pay more than lip service to common decency among peoples as well as individuals. I can hear the adjutant saying, 'Decency in a tripe shop.'

That's what we want to maintain when we shoot down German bombers over the sea near our coast and suspect that some of the crew are alive.

Pilot Officer Leslie Barnes and Sergeant Brejcha were right. One member of the Dornier that they shot down survived. It was not the pilot but the flight engineer, Waldemar Blaschyk, who parachuted into the sea. He was rescued by a vessel from Great Yarmouth and became a prisoner of war.[100] Fourteen civilians had been killed by the German bombs on Lowestoft. A few months later, Sergeant Brejcha himself died when a Tiger Moth he was ferrying back to Coltishall crashed into the sea near Southwold.

Myers also had an eye and ear for the lighter conversations on the station too.

My Love

The Squadron Leader in charge of administration, Peter Price, who would have been an Air Vice-Marshal by now if his accent had been refined, told us last night

[100]*Lowestoft Journal* February 22 2016

over a glass of whisky how he lost his first promotion. He had been drinking for some time in the mess bar, and spirits added a little zest to his natural wit.

Before the war he had been working in balloons when Viscount Trenchard, the man credited with being the father of the modern Royal Air Force, and a fellow senior officer, toured on an inspection with their wives. Price wanted to make an impression and give the women an exciting visit.

'I asked the ladies if they would like to get inside the balloon. When they were in, I undid some of the sandbags to give them the sensation of the balloon rising. But I undid too many and the balloon went up. It shot up 180 feet into the air. You should have heard those women scream!

'Trenchard remained silent. When I got the balloon down he looked at me with an icy glare and said, "What's your name?" "Price, sir," I replied. Then he said, "I'll see that you will never get promotion."'

Although he was overlooked for promotion, Price soon recovered from the farce with the officers' wives. He was given a job in the secret service and was sent to Germany to try to discover how many Zeppelins they were making, what their performance was, and for what purpose they were being built. So, Price was sent to pre-war Berlin to stay in a smart hotel and meet some key German contacts.

That was where Price's interest and expertise in balloons came into play again.

'On this trip I met this lovely bit of Austrian stuff in a hotel. She asked me to take her for a trip in a balloon. I said I hadn't got one but she told me we could hire one, which we did. Oh what a wonderful feeling! Lovely

warm evening. Blue sky fading into red and brown, the balloon floating in a gentle breeze, anywhere it pleased and this lovely Austrian girl inside. Soon she was naked. We landed miles and miles away, in Holland.'

Meanwhile, Margot Myers and her children stayed with their friends in the countryside near Moulins for three months. Within a few days the grocer and his trusty wife had smuggled clothes across the demarcation line in a box marked 'soap'. Fortunately, they were very isolated and Margot cycled everywhere. She was cautious about everyone and everything. Her friends were Pétainists themselves, but they had known Margot's family a long time and were completely trustworthy. Their children were sweet and soon adopted Robert and Anne as their own playmates. Although the free zone was less frightening than her life across the border in the occupied zone, there was a big question about whether the Germans would flood south to annexe the southern half of France.

In February 1941, Margot finally managed to get a message out to England, to the home of Geoff's mother in Oxfordshire. His friend John passed the news to Geoff at Coltishall. The message revealed that Margot and their two children had escaped safely across the border into the unoccupied zone, and that her intention was to try and travel to England via Lisbon.

March 15 1941

I am like a schoolboy striking off the days until the end of term, counting the hours and minutes that go by. I sometimes want time to stop, so that I can grip and control its course, perhaps at the end of the counting

I shall turn time inside out, wishing that I were back in February (when I got your message). It's all very silly. It would have been better if I had been a little more dispassionate and written to you regularly but I couldn't.

On February 6 I came into the mess for lunch from the aerodrome and was told by the telephone orderly that John had rung up. I felt the blood rushing to my cheeks. The boy said, 'the gentlemen told me it was urgent and you should ring him.' My legs seemed to run away with me as I went to the telephone. Sometime afterwards I drank in John's voice telling me that that you had crossed into unoccupied France and were at La Busserie, near Moulins. The grey fog which had been hovering for ten days suddenly lifted. The early spring day seemed to be lovely. I forgot the war for a few minutes. I felt just as I used to after a long night's work when I came into the bedroom and you awoke, switched on the lamp, rubbed your eyes and smiled.

Myers's colleagues in 257 understood the importance of his news from Moulins. His closest friends in the squadron had seen the strain he was under while he tried to stay cheerful for the sake of his job. The next day he was allowed to travel down to London to try to make arrangements for his family's onward transportation.

I saw the official at the prisoners of war department for the third time. He seemed pleasantly surprised and arranged to give the full details to the American authorities, so that you could gain facilities even if you did not have your passport with you. I booked passages by air from Lisbon to London and I telegraphed you to go and see John Elliott [their American journalist friend] in Vichy. I telegraphed to him.

Later I saw my friends at the *Daily Telegraph*, and with the help of the editor, sent telegrams to the correspondents in Lisbon and Madrid. I then telegraphed John Elliott again, telling him that they were helping and giving their addresses. A stream of telegrams started flowing back from the continent with encouraging messages.

On February 14 I received that wonderful telegram from Vichy, 'Margot getting necessary papers. Will leave soon possible. Is well. Sends love. Regards.'

Myers wrote this letter in March 1941 and so it was already more than a month since he had heard that his family were safe in the countryside near Moulins. His desperation to see his family had rather run away with him. Escaping a second time, this time through unoccupied France, was not as easy as he hoped. Margot was cautious and uncertain. She knew that she needed to keep one step ahead of the Germans, but she had no idea how to proceed next.

Margot was alone with her two young children with no one to advise her about the least risky way to reach safety. She felt very isolated and stayed in Moulins for three months, wrestling with how to get to Spain safely.

For Geoffrey the waiting continued, but there was still a war to be fought.

March 15 1941

I started counting the minutes. There was little excitement at the aerodrome except for an attack by enemy planes when our squadron was carrying out night-flying practice. Just before midnight, when I was watching the boys circling round the aerodrome before

landing, there was a quick burst of machine gun fire, followed by several others. The flare path was fully lighted and the moon was so brilliant that you could see the aerodrome from 15,000 feet above the ground. A flight sergeant ran up to us. His lips were quivering as he blurted out, 'They've shot down one of our boys. I saw him dive, just after the machine gun fire. He must have crashed over there.'

He could not hold his arm straight. He was trembling too much. As we were looking out over the aerodrome, the station commander, who was with us, sounded the alarm and ordered us to take cover. Just as we were going into the shelters, showers of incendiary bombs fell through and around the hangars. Our new medical officer and I ran to one of the hangars to put out the incendiaries which were burning near an aircraft. We tackled the job like the amateurs that we were. I felt rather ashamed of doing so clumsily what civilians in and around London did with expert experience.

In the dark, after we had extinguished incendiaries in the hangar, I fell into an open sump for water piping and twisted my ankle. I found it rather difficult, hobbling along to put out the other incendiaries. One was burning away just outside the hanger in a patch of half-mown grass. Having no sand handy, I dug up the wet clay with my fingers and smothered it. I almost felt as if I were having a game with you, my little Robert, digging mud pies.

Our boys were still flying around the aerodrome but all lights had been extinguished. I looked around, expecting the high explosive bombs to follow any moment. I suppose the attacking planes must have been light aircraft for they dropped no big stuff at all.

All our boys had landed after the raid. There had been some near misses but the flight sergeant, in his excitement, had just imagined things. The incendiaries had done no damage at all. There had only been about forty of them and they had all been put out within about five minutes.

For Margot life was not easy at La Busserie. She travelled down to Vichy several times to try to find a way forward, and the journey entailed a bike ride in the dark, just before dawn, followed by a bus. On other occasions, she would wait for hours in a local cafe three kilometres away, just to make a simple phone call. For important documents she travelled the seven kilometres to Tronget where the postmistress was compassionate and the family was finally able to have their identity card photographs taken.

Life was not easy for her friend Madeleine either. Money was tight but she never complained about the three extra people in her house. Her husband Pierre had a position in the Vichy government and Margot was never sure exactly where he stood politically. He supported Pétain but raised no objection to his wife sheltering a runaway family with a Jewish husband and father.

'At La Busserie they would speak of Pétain with great admiration. It was very hard for me to keep my mouth shut! I would have so liked to listen to the radio broadcasts from London, but that was out of the question. Here they would listen to Radio-Vichy on which Pétain's every move and pronouncement was described in full.'[101]

[101]Memoirs of Margot Myers translated by her daughter, Anne

Geoff had no idea whether his family was safe but at least he had a reasonable grasp on what was happening in France. Margot, on the other hand, was completely in the dark about the progress of the war, apart from any propaganda she picked up.

Once or twice Madeleine's husband gave Margot a lift into Vichy when he returned from a few days at home, back to his work for the Vichy government. 'When I happened to meet his colleagues or friends I would overhear their most pro-Pétain conversations.'

Vichy was full of people trying to sort out their vital paperwork, 'In the offices where I waited in line, I met families from Central Europe who were clamouring for resident permits, exit permits, visas. I could feel everyone's anxiety. The answers that they received were generally discouraging. One had to wait, wait, wait.'

Vichy was a magnet for Jewish refugees from all over Europe. By the time Margot arrived there, thousands had already been expelled from the city and anti-Semitic propaganda was openly allowed. In 1941, the anti-Jewish activity in Vichy was stepped up. A known anti-Semite was put in charge of a campaign against the Jews including mail interception and telephone tapping.[102]

As Lisbon had been earmarked as the safest exit point to the United Kingdom, Margot Myers eventually decided to travel from Moulins to the Portuguese Consulate in Lyons. She had to secure an exit permit to leave Vichy, France, a permit to enter Spain and also a visitor's permit for Portugal. But first she needed US dollars. Her first attempt was greeted with a cry of 'impossible' from a grumpy bank cashier. On her second

[102]Audrey Mallett, University of Concordia thesis 2016

visit another cashier was more sympathetic, especially when he heard the word, 'England'. The man did not say anything but secretly gave Margot an address where she might find the currency she needed.

In an office in a Vichy hotel room, she found two men, 'They figured out themselves how much I would need to get to Lisbon and they accepted my francs without comment. It was Mother. Mother who always took care of everything, who had provided the money and had even found a way for me to receive it at Madeleine's house.'

Now, armed with her dollars, Margot made her way to the Portuguese Embassy. It was shuttered and closed. It was too small, she was told, to let refugees in. They would be overwhelmed. When the consul finally turned up very late, he saw the crowd and laughed, telling them that he was not receiving anyone that day. Then he slammed the door in their faces.

Margot was desperate but a kind stranger among the disappointed crowd suggested that she try the Americans. This was all new to Margot. To her surprise, on arrival at the American Consulate, she learnt that the USA was representing the British. The Americans were helpful and practical. They would help her.

In Coltishall, Norfolk, Geoffrey Myers received news that he was to be posted away to Martlesham Heath, just across the border in Suffolk, as assistant station intelligence officer. On two previous occasions he had been offered promotion to a station role but had turned it down so that he could stay with his squadron.

I had effectively been barring my own way to promotion but I did not think it mattered, as my work

with the squadron seemed as useful as any. This time, Group took it out of my hands and put a posting through. Most of my friends in the squadron had been posted, and in a short while Cowboy Blatchford would probably leave to command a station of his own. If you came back, there was more chance of seeing you at a station. I was too happy at the thought that perhaps I would see you again soon for anything else to matter.

Just after Myers was promoted and moved south a few miles to Martlesham Heath, Pilot Officer David Hunt rejoined 257 Squadron. He had finally been released from the Burns Unit at East Grinstead and, after some rehabilitation, was looking forward to seeing his old friends. But, so much had changed, as his wife recalled, *'Geoffrey, the intelligence officer, had been posted away and Jimmy Cochrane, the Canadian, and David Coke, whom he had most hoped to find, were abroad.'*

The mess was full of strangers but then *'Peter Blatchford came in, a Canadian who had visited David in hospital, and distinguished himself soon after, and the squadron he had just joined, in a wonderful encounter with the Italians. We were glad to see him, and to be allowed to talk at last. And here was Stanford Tuck, the squadron leader who was so much in the press that he had begun to creep into the more relevant adverts; and a wonderful blonde who soon bore him away. Certainly, it was a brand-new squadron.'*

Hunt had been hurried back to his squadron but was still not fit enough to fly. He was not needed on ground duties and so, quite quickly, David and Terry Hunt were moved on by the RAF to another station.

Myers was desperate for his wife to also be on the move. Writing in March, her husband realised that escaping the unoccupied zone was more complex and uncertain than he had understood.

I began to get uneasy again when I had no more news for a fortnight. On my birthday I received a note from my friend in London enclosing a telegram from our friends in Clermont-Ferrand. I then realised that I had been hoping for your return too early. I had to wait for six weeks. I have struck off ten days since then.

I have watched the spectre of France and Britain over the blockade.[103] I see no prospect of the blockade being lifted sufficiently to satisfy the Vichy government, for Vichy must follow Berlin in this or crash. It is appalling to feel that the blockade may be instrumental in preventing you from coming home and may bring those I love to the verge of starvation. It is appalling, especially as I know I must support it, because I feel it is one of our most powerful weapons.

Increasingly, Myers found comfort and messages in books, including the Bible. His favourite seemed to be Richard Llewellyn's *How Green Was My Valley*. But, as the amount of news from Margot increased, he replaced the imaginary world of books with the reality that his family was on the way home. Not that Margot and his children were free to travel yet, and any travel through Free France for a family with Jewish blood was potentially fraught with difficulties. But progress was being made.

March 17 1941

My little world has suddenly been filled with joy. When I walk, I feel as if I am stepping on billowy clouds

[103]The British blockade was part of the economic war with Germany. It used the Navy to try to block supplies of essential items like food, metals and coal.

filled with sunlight. The yellow buds on the hawthorn have been winking to me and the pine trees have been whispering words of hope. Good God, it is all so wonderful that I am overwhelmed by my own joy. I am so thankful for this blessing that everything is surging up in my veins and pumping laughter into my eyes. I will not, for all that, forget the misery of thousands around me, and I will try to be less selfish, less conceited and more tolerant.

There was a letter in my box this morning from the *Daily Telegraph*. I didn't know where to take it to open it. I cut the envelope carefully so as not to spoil anything inside, just as if I were unpacking a silk dress. The telegram was from Lisbon and said, 'Mrs Myers now received Portuguese and Spanish visas, awaits only exit visa.'

Until that moment I had always wondered what people meant when they talked of one's heart jumping into one's mouth. As I read the telegram, something went 'bump' above my stomach and I had difficulty in swallowing. It was probably my breakfast. I did not know whether I had received good news or bad. I thought that perhaps you were having difficulty with your exit permit and that, in spite of the visas, you might not be allowed to leave. I could not dismiss this thought during my work this morning.

My loved ones, I can start thinking of our meeting. I am bound up in you, and you are bound up in me. You have been with me despite this year of separation, but my thoughts have been filled with anguish.

I think it is a good thing for us all to try and remain cheerful. Your mother taught me that. I often think of her. Her son is a prisoner in Germany and now you are

leaving the country with her grandchildren. I will not forget what she has done for us all and I hope I shall live to bring her happiness in her old age. If Daddy is not alive, Robert and Anne, remember what he wanted to do and try to do it for her.

A friend said, 'Hello, I'm going to make you drunk tonight. I've got some news for you about your wife who hopes to be back soon. She's asking for your address.' The words would not go in, and went buzzing around my head like a swarm of bees let loose. He saw that I was dazed and repeated it all with a broad grin. I phoned John who read the telegram out to me, stating you hoped to leave in a fortnight.

One of the older officers was a confidante, and when Myers told him about his family he said:

> **'So you have got your private troubles. You must have been going through a pretty hard time. I would never have guessed it. You always seemed to me to be cheerful about the mess.'**
> **I was gratified because I had succeeded in doing what I had set out to do. It has helped me a great deal because by dint of being cheerful I have strengthened myself and gained optimism.**

Chapter Fifteen

March 17 1941

My Family,

My excitement is unbounded. You are coming home. You are really coming home. John has phoned me through a telegram. You expect to leave on Monday and be at Lisbon at the end of the month. Oh Joy of Joys. All the heaviness that has been pent up in me is dispersing. My little Robert, perhaps I shall see you soon. You will be a boy now. All the baby part of you will have disappeared. A little man of many travels. My darling Anne, I have tried to imagine you growing and have looked into the last little face your Mummy sent me a year ago when you were photographed on the steps at Beaurepaire. You are lovely, my little daughter.

Oh my Lovvy, you are bringing the children home. They will go back one day to see their Grandmother who has had to see them go. I have found a little house for us, and for perhaps a short respite we shall be able to live together again. I am overwhelmed by a great joy.

In Lyon, Margot, Robert and Anne were given the necessary travel papers by the Americans and she was able to buy train tickets from Thomas Cook, who were still operating. They had been staying with Madeleine at La Busserie for three months now. Margot was filled with a mixture of sadness, relief, gratitude and fear for what lay ahead, as the family finally left their refuge. Madeleine went out of her way to ensure that the Myers family would not go hungry on their long journey, baking cakes and even killing a chicken.

The train tickets that Margot Myers had obtained were for travel to Madrid via Toulouse. The first leg of the journey was uneventful despite having to find a hotel in Toulouse in the dark. In Barcelona, they were amazed to be met by a man from Thomas Cook in a magnificent cap who looked after them well. The onward journey to Madrid the next day, however, was a nightmare. The train was packed to the rafters with people piled on top of each other. Some people were even sleeping in the luggage racks. People argued about seats and her children always seemed to need the toilet. The ticket collector had to climb over mountains of people to check their documents. When Robert urgently needed the toilet, Margot found a woman squatting on it who resolutely refused to move. After what seemed an interminable wait, the woman finally succumbed to pressure but, once Robert had relieved himself, she swiftly squatted back down again, to the utter frustration of the rest of the queue. Despite the terrible overcrowding, on the whole, the other travellers, all equally desperate, were kind to her children.

Margot was very disturbed when she encountered Jewish refugees on the way. They all looked deeply anxious. At the border she was frightened when she was rudely searched by a Spanish official. 'An old witch had the assignment of frisking me. She had me enter a little booth and searched me all over, even under my skirts.'[104]

[104]Memoirs of Margot Myers translated by her daughter, Anne

But Margot had nothing to hide and was allowed on her way. As the overcrowding eased the journey became more comfortable and the children were in good spirits. Robert still has a childhood memory of Spanish children begging in Madrid, 'Anne and I gave them our sandwiches, all the food we had left.'[105]

Margot, however, was fearful that something could still go badly wrong.

In Madrid she met with the *Daily Telegraph* correspondent who gave her some reassurance. Finally, Margot was able to send a cable to her husband in England telling him that she was safe and heading for Lisbon. Geoff had booked his family plane tickets from Lisbon to London but they were 'preference' tickets not 'priority' tickets. Margot was horrified when she learnt there were already scores of people in the priority queue. 'I was so excited when the Air Ministry said that my family was a priority but I soon realised that others were Priority Plus.'[106] She understood that she would never get on a plane and that the only route back to Britain was by sea.

Margot felt stranded, trapped in Lisbon. The consular authorities told her that a boat home was her last chance. If she didn't take that opportunity, the consul could no longer take any responsibility for her and her family. It was a difficult decision. About half the convoys were being sunk at the time, but being stranded without consular protection was equally perilous. Margot sent an urgent message to her husband asking for advice. Myers made enquiries. The risk of staying in

[105]Interview with Robert Myers, February 2020
[106]Margot Myers memoir, translated by her daughter, Anne

Lisbon without support was significant but so was the hazardous journey home by sea.

The *Daily Telegraph* correspondent and his Spanish wife became good and helpful friends to Margot. Unfortunately, the Myers children fell ill. Robert was particularly sick and Margot was worried that he would not be fit to travel. As he recovered from one illness, he suffered from another, this time a serious ear infection, 'I was terribly worried because he was in pain and I feared the worst.'

Margot just did not know what the safest plan was, 'Portugal would not want to keep us indefinitely and there was always the German menace. What to do? I knew that ships were being sunk every day. But refusing to leave meant burning our bridges.'[107]

Eventually she received a telegram from England, 'Geoff, who had at first been as worried as I was, advised me to leave all the same.'

News came through that a boat for the ever-growing number of stranded British subjects was finally available. But then the boat was cancelled and all British subjects were told to wait for two further months. Instead of disappointment, Margot felt relief. Now there was a good chance that Robert would have time to recover and be well again, and that the family could catch the delayed boat.

The children got better as they waited. They lived in a tiny pensión in Estoril and Margot made friends with women from France, Spain and England who were all, in their different ways, waiting, just as she was.

[107]Memoirs of Margot Myers translated by her daughter, Anne

June 28 1941

My darling,

It is just three months since you arrived in Lisbon. Now I am sure you are on your way home. I am again full of hope, confident that I shall soon be seeing you. My feelings are like the waters of a shallow lake. I am only able to glide along the surface, not daring to dip my paddle below for fear of stirring up the muddy bottom. I am trying to suppress my excitement and keep my equanimity.

I will not tell the family that I am sure you are on the sea in a convoy from Gibraltar. They need not go through unnecessary worry. They will know when you are back. It has been wonderful to write you letters which you have received for the last three months. Our letters have been freely written, but there are hundreds of questions I want to ask you, hundreds of things I want to say.

I have had to damp down my feelings for so many weeks now that I am determined not to let them bubble over until you are home. The period of deferred hope is over.

Dangers were ever-present and Geoffrey often heard bad news about pilots he had met earlier in the war. Hugh had been the shy twenty-year-old worried about his wife at the social events in Coltishall.

Hugh has been killed in a flying accident. His little wife will be crying her eyes out tonight. I am seventy miles away and can do nothing. Hugh was posted from the squadron to an operational training unit where he seemed safe. He was upset at leaving the squadron but his wife was delighted. She had four months' happiness with him. They danced every night at the mess. She loved

dancing. Now he has gone, and I can't do anything for the girl.

I have been praying for your safety, and praying too, to be as brave as you are.

God bless You and the Children.

Eventually the Myers family left Lisbon on the SS Avoceta, a small, former British-built cruise ship built in 1923 and bound for Gibraltar. The journey was full of alarms. Once, soon after departure, Margot was sitting peacefully in the lounge in a seat from which she could see her cabin door, having just put the children to bed. It was eerily quiet. A woman suddenly burst into the lounge exclaiming they were under attack.

Margot desperately hurried to the cabin and, with great difficulty, dragged the sleepy children plus their life jackets to the dining hall. Robert still remembers being scared, 'Everybody crammed into the dining hall. Dead silence. Then Anne woke up and began screaming. They had trouble calming her down. I apparently sensed the danger and was very quiet but remember being very frightened'.[108]

They had been attacked by an enemy aircraft, but working out the exact truth was difficult. Rumours circulated fast on the small boat and the crew were under strict orders not to say anything. All Margot knew was that her children were in danger.

Fortunately, they arrived safely. 'I have forgotten the exact details of our arrival. All I can remember is the long wait and our climbing down into the launches that would take us to the big ship. I was much moved when

[108]Robert Myers memoir

a group of young British men and women began to sing gravely in honour of the captain who had piloted us to safety. Years later I learnt that the Avoceta had sunk during one of her subsequent voyages.'[109]

Indeed, Margot, Robert and Anne had been very lucky. On September 25 1941, just a couple of months later, the SS Avoceta was attacked near the Azores and sank. 123 people on board lost their lives. It was one of a twenty-five strong convoy, HG-73, from Gibraltar. All told, nine ships in the convoy were sunk; one of the worst losses of the entire Atlantic campaign.

The second ship from Gibraltar, the Scythia, was an altogether grander affair, much larger and more comfortable. It was a liner for the Cunard company. But Margot was wise enough to know that size merely made the Scythia a more attractive target for the enemy.

Two weeks after Margot had arrived a convoy was finally formed in Gibraltar. Before they set sail for the United Kingdom all passengers spent two weeks being trained for the worst. A sergeant major relentlessly, sometimes brutally, drilled everyone, including children, in evacuation procedures in case the boat sank. Some of the passengers could not speak a word of English. It was a very nerve-wracking journey. Bomb scares were a regular occurrence and the risk of mines or attacks by submarines was obvious to Margot. In case the family was separated, or worse, she fastened waterproof plastic bags round the necks of the children which contained their identity and addresses.

[109]Notes from Margot Myers translated by her daughter, Anne

One very refined elderly English woman summed up their predicament when, in a cut-glass accent, she said, rather curtly, to the bullying sergeant major, 'If I understand you correctly, we run the risk of an air attack, a submarine attack, or we can be blown up by mines.'[110]

Myers knew that boat travel was very risky. He had seen or heard of enough convoys being attacked by Germans to know that the passage home was not assured.

July 1 1941

I have not been able to tell you what I have been going through during the past months. It would have been foolish to dwell on it. Every time that my hopes of your return were dashed I thought of you, my Tite, and your courage. I have also thought of all the others who were going through torture and misery without hope on earth. I then felt ashamed. Now you are on the sea. I have learnt my lesson.

I used to have a smug and comfortable feeling when thinking of Beaurepaire and the safety that it afforded you in all circumstances, but the war swept by there when I thought that no such thing could happen. Now you have left that place, which once spelt security for me, and you are on the sea.

His colleagues were not always sensitive to the dangers the Myers family were facing at sea.

A colleague at Group, whose French wife is still in occupied France, asked me whether I had agreed to your going by sea. I told him I had. Then he started saying, 'I

[110]Interview with Janet Willis 1981

wouldn't do that. It is so dangerous by sea... torpedoes and things...' I interrupted him, saying, 'Goodnight. I'm off,' and left him.

What else did he think I had in my thoughts? Of course I have followed the statistics of enemy sinkings and I can't get the danger of it all out of my head. Whatever happens, my Family, I feel we were right in deciding to take the risk. If we all go under in the venture I will go on believing in God and accept what comes. You have helped me face things fearlessly, my Love. I am almost calm.

Before the end of the letter there is a reminder that the RAF were still in a bitter war.

The Polish squadrons have just lost their wing commander. He was a favourite among the British pilots too. On an offensive sweep two days ago his aircraft was hit by anti-aircraft fire and he crashed in flames into the sea. He had been waiting for twenty months for news of his wife he had left behind in Poland. Only last week he had received a message saying that his wife had escaped from Poland to Siberia and was on her way to join him.

This was one of the constant reminders of the value of leadership. Having seen the impact of poor leadership under Harkness, and the positive difference made by men like Tuck, Brothers and Blatchford, it was an area whose significance was now fully understood by Myers.

The American Eagle Squadron [one of three squadrons populated by American volunteer pilots] is with us now. The politicians realise their propaganda value. They are not yet a good squadron... they need an energetic and bold squadron leader but they have got a tired man who knows what is wanted but cannot make them do it. He is a kind man, full of consideration for his pilots, who

has a look of sorrow at the back of his eyes. He is a thinking man. Possibly he thinks too much.

Sometimes, too, it was as if Fighter Command had learned none of the lessons from the inadequacies of Squadron Leader Harkness and a handful of other leaders. A year after the Battle of Britain, the squadron they shared the aerodrome with was going through very similar problems. Like Harkness, their squadron leader had been transferred from a training squadron to an operational unit. Their desperate intelligence officer told Myers the story.

The squadron leader was too vain to notice that the pilots despised him. He insisted that he knew all about flying tactics and would not listen to suggestions. He went up with his squadron on a practice flight. The squadron took off in ragged formation. An hour later they came down, white with rage and shaken. One sergeant pilot had dived from 4,000 feet into the sea. His aircraft had disappeared. There was no hope. The pilots started cursing under their breath, 'What a clot Maclean is. We won't go up with him again, no bloody fear. It's suicide… he's crazy.'

The next day, Maclean was relieved of his command. Myers could not help thinking back to the early days of the Battle of Britain and of the pilots that 257 had lost under the command of Harkness. But his family, now on the precarious escape route home, were always in his thoughts. He still had not told the rest of the family in Oxfordshire.

I have not told them that you are on the sea. It would be unnecessary worry for them, especially for Mother. This evening, while I was at the farm next door, the telephone bell rang and everything in me hurt, especially

my throat. I had to steady myself while the call was being answered. I thought it might bring me news but it was a local farmer ringing up. Perhaps I will have to wait for a fortnight before receiving news. I will be patient and I will remember what others are going through.

Margot, Robert and Anne were already on their way when this letter was written. They left Gibraltar one late evening during a blackout. It was a very mixed group of people on board – Polish, French and Italian as well as British. All of them had a British connection but not all could speak the language.

The journey was tense and difficult. The boat was so crowded there was very little space. Passengers ranged from refugees and injured servicemen to elderly, aristocratic spinsters who had been living on the Riviera.

The ship was very hot but there was a chronic water shortage and it was rationed. The wealthy spinsters from the Riviera, relatives of the Duke of Westminster, were desperate for a bath, water rationing or not. Margot heard the steward say, 'They should be on their hands and knees saying their prayers and here they are, clamouring for their baths.'[111]

At night, Margot would not get undressed in case there was an emergency alarm and she needed to be ready at a moment's notice. Early in the voyage from Gibraltar, the alarm had gone off and there was a general sense of panic and heightened anxiety. 'We had put on our life preservers and were waiting. The children were good. We heard some muffled explosions and I thought I heard the boat shudder.'[112]

[111]Interview with Janet Willis, 1981
[112]Margot Myers memoirs, translated by her daughter, Anne

The two refugee ships that had left Gibraltar sailed in parallel. They were escorted by an aircraft carrier, the Furious, and two or three destroyers and, after the alarm at night, which had been caused by increased German submarine presence, a cruiser was added to the convoy. 'Looking through the porthole I saw, sailing beside us, a magnificent cruiser. It was the Edinburgh. Its presence comforted me.' The convoy avoided submarine lanes as best as it could. Planes from the aircraft carrier warily circled overhead, almost continuously.

Despite the pressure, everyone helped each other whatever their background. They were all facing the same risks, the same uncertainties. Anxious though she was, Margot felt lucky in some ways when she looked at the injured servicemen or thought about those who spoke little English and had nowhere to go when they reached Dover. One Polish woman with an English husband had five children. They were, Margot thought, a strange crowd of people all thrown together by the randomness of war. One day she heard an English sailor, gazing at the refugees, say coldly, 'To think we are risking our lives for these people.'

Inevitably, the Scythia seethed with gossip. There were rumours of spies on board. One night, Margot returned to find her cabin a terrible mess. The authorities had been looking for a secret radio transmitter.

Myers, meanwhile, had been following the convoy with concern. He heard it had been attacked. He vividly imagined his wife and children were at the bottom of the sea. He desperately rang whoever he could think of, to find out more. Geoffrey was relieved to discover he had been badly misinformed about the name of the ship that his family had left Gibraltar on, and that he had been unnecessarily distraught.

July 10 1941

Talk about being flattened out! Last night I thought that you must have actually arrived at either Liverpool or the Clyde. It all happened because I phoned a friend at Group asking him if he could give me information about your ship. I imagined that you had left Lisbon about the 19 and I gave this date. A few days ago, he asked the naval liaison officer at Fighter Command about the ship. The news was grand. The convoy was north of Ireland and would split into three. You were due to dock at Liverpool, Carlisle or Oban in two- or three-days' time.

Last night, after dinner, my friend told me that you had arrived. I felt like a morning breeze. My feet were light and my head was dizzy with excitement. It had become known in the mess that you had arrived, so we had drinks to celebrate it. Two or three bottles of Graves were fetched from the mess cellar. The wine was filthy, but I didn't care. I did not need a drop and drank little because I wanted to be fresh for the morning.

The morning was a let-down. Several phone calls to friends produced no further news. No one had heard from Margot or from the ship. Then a letter arrived for Myers.

Instead of a telegram, I received a letter from you dated June 25. So your ship was waiting somewhere before sailing. Obviously, you were in Gibraltar when I thought you were on the way back. I phoned the Air Ministry Civil Airways Department to see if they had any news. Their information was that you were still in

Gibraltar, so I keep on wondering if you are there now, or on the sea. I'm going through it all over again. Just a bit of bungling on my part that has cost me a great deal. I must hide all the thoughts of last night. I must not look at the little cot too much. I must get back to that cold storage feeling, because I must concentrate on my work and not show my disappointment.

In fact, his family was closer than he imagined. One evening, after they had been sailing for two weeks, Margot spotted a rocky island and asked a sailor if it was England. 'That's the beginning of it,' the man said. The next morning, they saw two battleships coming out to welcome them, 'They took my breath away and I felt deeply moved,' she recalled.[113] It was probably the most dangerous part of the journey with all the mines but Margot felt curiously safe. That night she undressed for the first time on her long journey.

The following day the boat headed up the Clyde. No one in the shipyards was working because it was a Sunday. Margot was surprised. There was a war on, she thought, and Britain was short of ships.

'At last we were on British soil! Everything happened as though we were arriving under normal conditions. They calmly checked our passports and luggage. Ever since the fall of France, in June 1940, I had lived in an atmosphere of fear, ignoring what the next day would bring. I had endured administrative complications, difficulties of travel. I had needed to fight and hold my own among the crowds. I had witnessed all these lost people who seemed to be running around in circles with

[113]Margot Myers memoirs, translated by her daughter, Anne

no exit in sight. For the first time since the fall, I felt reassured. I was in a free country.'[114]

To Margot, fresh from the brightness of Lisbon and Madrid, wartime Glasgow seemed a dismal, grey city. She found a small city centre hotel and was so delighted, and astonished, to have arrived safely that she gave the porter a ten-shilling note for a tip. He was so shocked he said, 'Haven't you got anything smaller?'

The next morning there was a knock on Margot's hotel door. Geoff Myers had travelled all night to finally be reunited with his family. There was a tremendous electricity in the air. Everyone seemed to be crying. Robert remembers his father lifting his mother off her feet in a huge embrace, 'I was amazed how strong he was.'[115] Margot had talked to her children often about their father in England and had explained that the whole point of the long and dangerous journey was to join him. Now they understood. Myers recalled, 'I wondered if the children would recognise me?'[116] Margot, Robert and Anne jumped up and clung round his neck. 'It has been like that with the children ever since.'

Margot and Geoff had not seen each other for nearly eighteen months, between March 1940 and July 1941. The children had changed hugely in that time. Margot remembers 'a hugely emotional moment.'[117]

The reunited family went first to Edinburgh. On a bus, Margot was talking in French to Anne and a woman leaned over and gave Anne a silver 3d bit for luck. From Scotland they moved to Ipswich where there

[114]Memoirs of Margot Myers translated by her daughter, Anne
[115]Interview with Author, 2020
[116]Interview with Author, 1981
[117]Memoirs of Margot Myers, translated by her daughter, Anne

was a house waiting for them. Alan Birtwhistle, the new intelligence officer at 257, was very helpful. Soon, Myers began telling his wife about the Battle of Britain and what had happened to his squadron. He gave her the unposted letters. Margot was astonished.

Margot was desperate to reconnect with her family in occupied France and to let them know that she and the children were safe. Robert and Anne missed their time with their grandmother. Margot was both horrified and relieved to discover that soon after she and her children had escaped, they had been betrayed by a local to the occupying Nazis.

The diary and letters were redundant now. Geoff was in direct contact with his family and had no need to write anything further in the notebooks for the family to read after the war. He waited six weeks and then wrote one last entry.

August 27 1941

Six weeks of dream. Mummy is at my side, my little ones, and you are sleeping a few yards away. Mummy has asked me to go on writing so you know how things were. I want you to both realise first how Mummy and I are utterly soaked in thankfulness for this deliverance. Since we have been together again some people have talked about fate, others about providence, and others about God. If your ship had been sunk, we should still have been dependent on these same forces.

Chapter Sixteen

No one described the reality of the Battle of Britain better than Terry Hunt, who in 1942 wrote *Pilot's Wife's Tale: the diary of a camp-follower.* As she emphasised when we met near her flat in Victoria in 1982, 'It was a queer golden time. The world seemed full of lights. They were golden boys too. You met people once or twice and then they were dead. Now they seem such little boys, such boys.'[118]

Terry Hunt was right. Although every day young men were killed defending their country in the Battle of Britain, there was an unreal quality to those months too. It was summer and the days were long and bright. Below them, as they flew, were the green and brown fields of Kent and Sussex, covered with hop fields and hay bales, orchards and oast houses. The pilots could see small villages with their pubs and churches, and sometimes a cricket field. It was a constant reminder of the country they were fighting for.

The pilots were young, in their early twenties mostly, but a few as young as eighteen. Geoffrey Myers, being a few years older, would survey his squadron and think, 'They looked so young and so innocent, as if they had come straight from school to war.'[119]

[118]Interview with Author, 1981
[119]Interview with Author

For most of the young men, war was an escape from the factory or the office, the classroom or the shop. It was as if they had been given a Ferrari or a Maserati to drive, although Spitfires and Hurricanes were bigger, faster and infinitely more dangerous. On top of that, the pilots of Fighter Command were paid, some more generously than in their civilian lives, and they were well fed and watered.

There was an intensity about everything, whole lives compressed into a few months or even weeks. Friendships were deep, as only those whose survival sometimes depended on the pilot in the Hurricane alongside him could fully understand. Alcohol was in plentiful supply and some young men would drink in a week a quantity that would have taken months to down in peacetime.

In war, inevitably, relationships with the opposite sex were speeded up too, as the pre-war boundaries faded away. The brave fighter pilots in their uniforms were very attractive to women and, if you didn't know whether you would be alive tomorrow, why wait for anything, including sex? Some women, too, had already lost a fiancé or a partner earlier in the war and they didn't want to risk losing a second loved one. So courtships were short and marriages often happened quickly.

This sense of grabbing at happiness echoes in the diary of the chaplain at RAF Duxford near Cambridge, when he described how his close friend, Pilot Officer Peter Watson, talked to him frankly about his relationship with a woman in Norwich. 'Watson said, "What does it matter? I shall be killed anyway; if not killed, I shall be maimed; there won't be much left to live with." We talked and walked for a long time, very frankly and about many things with a directness that

I never wanted to talk to any young man about. We both of us smelled death. So, he feels the hurry to do things while there is time...'[120] Peter Watson was killed a few weeks later.

As the emotional charge of the letters from Myers to his family convey, separation and danger only added to the overall intensity. The letters would often shift suddenly between his profound and private concerns for his family to his more public responsibility and fear for the young men in his charge. Geoff saw all too clearly how that sometimes unreal world of young pilots, the world 'full of lights,' could come to a sudden and lethal end. Myers was living on a daily basis with two different types of deep and powerful relationships.

Terry Hunt's life was wrenched out of that 'queer golden time' when her young husband was shot down and badly burned just a few weeks into the Battle of Britain. When she saw his terrible injuries, she thought, *'He himself was something brand new and very real.'* Although David was not blind, as originally seemed likely, his wife spent many long months caring for him. In 1943, her book was turned into a radio play starring Hugh Burden and Wendy Hiller, but in the radio adaptation the pilot was not burned 'because it [would not be] good for recruitment.'[121]

In a letter to Geoff Myers, Terry Hunt added, 'David was indignant when the BBC said he should be wounded in a more amusing way. I think that was how they put it. He said he would be burned or nothing; but finally had

[120]Diaries of Guy Mayfield, edited by Carl Warner, *Life and Death in the Battle of Britain* (Imperial War Museum, 2018)
[121]Interview with Author

to settle for a couple of broken ankles so as not to put people off.'[122]

For the pilots of 257 Squadron, reintegrating to civilian life was never going to be easy. Nothing was ever going to be as exciting as flying a Spitfire or Hurricane in combat. Most of the pilots had reached the pinnacle of their lives at twenty-one or twenty-two. As Terry Hunt observed of her husband, 'David said he'd rather do war again – including the burning up – than be an edge tool worker in a ghastly place like Wolverhampton.'[123]

David and Terry Hunt never did return to Wolverhampton. As a Guinea Pig under Sir Archibald McIndoe at East Grinstead, David had extensive surgery. After a year he managed to fly again, although he never flew in combat. Through the rest of the war he co-ordinated vital defence systems including radar, before leaving the Air Force as a flight lieutenant in 1945.

Terry Hunt recorded her feelings at the end of the war. 'It was four o'clock in the morning on VE Day in Cardiganshire. The victory beacons were going out. I thought of those who weren't there to share that moment and then I realised that the golden years had gone, they had dried out with that fire.'[124]

David and Terry Hunt later divorced. David moved to New Zealand, where he died in 2000, sixty years after his almost fatal crash.

If Bob Stanford Tuck was a legend going into the Battle of Britain, he was even more famous afterwards, partly

[122]Letter to Geoff Myers, 1980
[123]Interview with Author
[124]Interview with Author, 1981

for his exceptional work in welding 257 into a more than capable squadron. *The Times* wrote of his fame, 'In the face of constant death he preserved a lightness of heart, which was not simply bravura, but was allied to a precise and ruthlessly applied technical skill.'

In July 1941, Tuck – now a wing commander – moved from 257 to take command of the fighter squadrons at RAF Duxford in Cambridgeshire. Six months later, in January 1942, it looked like Tuck's legendary luck had finally run out. He had already moved on from Duxford to take charge of RAF Biggin Hill, just outside Bromley in Kent. Soon after, he was caught in cross-fire flying at low altitude close to Boulogne in northern France. His engine belched smoke and his windscreen was smeared with oil. Tuck was flying too low to be able to bail out, so he had no alternative but to crash-land in a French field.

The Immortal Tuck was immediately taken into custody. He was moved to the prison camp Stalag Luft III where he stayed for more than two years. Unsurprisingly, Tuck was part of the group that planned what became known as the Great Escape. But just before the actual escape, Tuck was moved from Stalag Luft III to a satellite camp called Belaria, six miles away on the other side of the local town, Sagan.

Bob Tuck and the others who were moved to Belaria, all of whom were suspected of actively planning an escape, cursed that they had missed the Great Escape by just a few days. In another way, however, this was Tuck's Luck working its magic again. Seventy-six men escaped in the Great Escape, and all but three were recaptured. Fifty prisoners were then executed by the Germans including Roger Bushell, the key architect of the plan. Given his own role in the escape team and his powerful personality, there is little doubt that Tuck would have also been killed by the Germans had he played an active part in the original plan.

Belaria was a bleak, isolated but well-guarded camp. Suddenly, at the end of January 1945, the prisoners were moved out of the camp and began marching through the deep snow in a south-westerly direction. At a farm in Upper Silesia, where the marching prisoners stopped for the night, Tuck and a fellow pilot, Zbishek Kustrzyński, managed to fool their German captors and escape. They worked their way east, supported largely by Russian slave labourers. They even fought alongside the Russians for a time. It was a long, tough journey, peppered with close encounters, but eventually the two escapers made it through Poland across the Russian border where they were able to phone the British Air Mission in Moscow. They were safe.

In 1949, Tuck finally retired from the RAF after an astonishing service career but he continued to exhibit his flying skills as a test pilot. Eventually, he retired from that too and in 1953 he became a mushroom farmer in Kent. He was successful in business but spent much of the rest of his life as what might be called a Battle of Britain 'professional', endlessly touring, lecturing and writing about the war. His lectures were sometimes in tandem with the famous German pilot, Adolf Galland. One of the quirks of war was that these two men became great friends. They holidayed together and Tuck became godfather to Galland's children. The irony was not lost on Tuck. When we interviewed him in 1984, in Ian Fleming's former property overlooking Sandwich Bay in Kent, he said, 'Many people think it is strange that we should be such good friends but when we met, we discovered we had a lot in common. Galland was never a Nazi, just a damned good pilot.'[125]

Some of the less high-profile pilots from 257 Squadron also stayed in the RAF in the years after the Battle of Britain. Sergeant Pilot Reg Nutter was called up on the outbreak of war and was moved to 257 Squadron after his training. He flew 112 operational flights with his squadron before being moved to the training school at Hullavington as an instructor and, early the next year, to a similar role in Medicine Hat, Canada. After three years in Canada, Nutter saw active service again over Germany and Holland in 1944–45, before being attached to the famous Desert Rats as they advanced through Germany. He was awarded a DFC on September 14 1945 and the citation read, 'This officer has completed numerous operations against the enemy in the course of which he has at all times displayed outstanding courage, fortitude and devotion to duty.'

After the war, Nutter moved back to Canada where he had already met and married a Canadian woman. He became a conductor on the Canadian Pacific Railway, before training as a teacher. He died in Calgary on December 9 2014 in his nineties.

The Canadian connection was also strong with other squadron pilots who had made less of a mark in the Battle of Britain. Charles Frizzell, who moved to Canada, and Jimmy Cochrane, both rather ignominiously dumped out of the Battle of Britain in the drunken car smash, continued with the RAF after they had recovered from their injuries.

[125]Interview with Author

Frizzell, after returning to action several months after the incident, was rapidly promoted. He served with 91 Squadron doing shipping recces up and down the Channel. In 1942–43 he served in North Africa with 152 Squadron. In June 1943, Charles was posted to command 1676 Fighter Defence Flight at Gibraltar. He retired from the RAF in 1946, eventually moving to Canada and becoming a teacher.

Over time, Frizzell became very disillusioned with what he called, 'a sort of bogus romantic cult that has been built up about the Battle of Britain,' but in the wider context he was clear. 'It was a war. I think that sometimes it is necessary for a small minority of people to do unpleasant things in the form of killing people so that justice might prevail for the majority.'[126]

Looking back, he thought that the Battle of Britain was something of a 'jolly'. He said, 'At night we were able to return to a comfortable mess or to divert ourselves with gin and gypsy girls – whose numbers were legion.'

Frizzell felt that 'war [was] a frightful folly. The tragedy is that when one is in touch with human folly, one is in touch with the infinite.'[127]

Arthur Charles 'Jimmy' Cochrane, Frizzell's fellow casualty in the car accident, was one of the 117 Canadians who flew in the Battle of Britain. Cochrane also returned to flying with conspicuous success. By 1942, he was leading 87 Squadron and, after some brilliant work in North Africa, was awarded the DFC. He and Frizzell were together in North Africa. The day

[126]BBC TV ' Inside Story: Missing' September 7 1980

[127]Letter to a memorabilia collector April 29 1977, copied to Author

after Cochrane received his DFC, March 31 1943, he crashed in the vicinity of Cap Bougeron, Tunis, and died.

Flying Officer John Claverly Martin, the twenty-six-year-old from Timaru in New Zealand, had been very lucky to survive the snowstorm at RAF Coltishall on January 1 1941 when Carl Capon had been killed. For several tense minutes, Myers and the rest of the squadron had mistakenly thought he was the one who had perished. But Martin did not benefit from his luck for long. He was posted missing in action over France a few months later on August 27 1941. He had died in a mid-air collision with a Hurricane from another squadron on his 131st operational sortie.

Overall, nearly 800 men who survived the Battle of Britain went on to be subsequently killed between 1940 and 1945 in other theatres of war. Only a few of 257 Squadron's Battle of Britain pilots managed to survive through five more years of the conflict.

Pilot Officer Kenneth Gundry, some of whose letters are in the Imperial War Museum, was wounded on October 12 1940 in combat over Deal and made an emergency landing at nearby RAF Detling. Eighteen months later, Gundry was shot down and killed in North Africa aged twenty-five. He is remembered on the Alamein Memorial.

Pilot Officer Francizek Surma, who had been shot down over Essex a day before the official end of the Battle of Britain on October 29 1940, had been lucky to survive. Surma had been caught in trees when he parachuted out at Moreton and, wearing a jacket with a German insignia, had only escaped a worse fate when he finally persuaded his rescuers that he was Polish and not German. A year later, Surma's luck ran out when he was shot down over the Channel on November 8 1941. Neither his body nor his aircraft were ever recovered.

Flying Officer David Coke, godson of Edward VIII and son of the Earl of Leicester from Holkham Hall, determinedly went back into action before the end of the Battle of Britain having had his finger shot off near the start. He returned to 257 before moving off to other squadrons. Flying with 80 Squadron in the Western Desert in Egypt, he was killed in action on December 9 1941, aged twenty-six, and buried in Libya. Coke was awarded a DFC on December 26 in the same year. The citation praised 'his skill and leadership.'

When Pete Brothers, the steadfast right-hand man of Stanford Tuck in the difficult days following the early disasters for 257, died at the age of ninety-one, his brilliant career meriting national newspaper obituaries. Brothers was credited with sixteen 'kills' in the Battle of Britain and, in 1943, was awarded the DSO. The citation noted, 'Wing Commander Brothers is a courageous and outstanding leader whose splendid example has inspired us all.'

After a distinguished career, including a spell in the Malaysian Emergency, he was made an Air Commodore in 1966. Brothers was always keen to remember those who had been less lucky than himself so, for many years, he was Chairman of the Battle of Britain Fighter Association.

Peter 'Cowboy 'Blatchford, perhaps the man that Myers respected and liked the most, succeeded Stanford Tuck as Commanding Officer of 257 Squadron. He leadership skills were not just apparent to Myers, as intelligence officer, but to Fighter Command more widely. In 1941, Cowboy was promoted to wing commander and he eventually returned to RAF Coltishall as wing leader in 1943. On May 3, he was leading his wing in an escort of British bombers attacking a power station in Amsterdam when he was involved in a desperate fight. Cowboy was hit and forced to ditch into the sea when his aircraft lost fuel. Despite several searches, Peter Blatchford's body was never found.

In 1979, nearly forty years after he was shot down over Kent, the body of Flight Lieutenant Hugh Beresford was finally lifted out of its muddy grave on the Isle of Sheppey. His Hurricane from 257 Squadron had crashed from around 20,000 feet and pieces of the plane were everywhere, but his body was surprisingly well preserved. His torso stayed intact, still held in place by the straps and harness. His legs had been smashed off at the knees but his flying boots were still neatly in place. Later the coroner noted a bullet hole in his back but could not be sure if that was the cause of Beresford's death.

As his colleague in 257, Sergeant Ronnie Forward, put it, 'Finding him was absolutely out of the blue. I can't believe he was found forty years later, buried in that muck. Terrific.'[128]

The coroner in 1979 said about Beresford, 'One of our national heroes. There were those who with undoubted courage and determination were prepared to sacrifice themselves for their country.'

Hugh Beresford was finally laid to rest in Brookwood Military Cemetery in Surrey with full military honours in November 1979. A fifteen-man escort party fired a three-volley salute and the band of RAF Cranwell played the 'Last Post'.

[128]Interview with Author

And what of our chronicler, Geoffrey Myers, and his family? Myers continued in the world of information and secrecy that he had been part of in France at the beginning of the war and then as an intelligence officer in Fighter Command. He was posted to the legendary code-breaking unit at Bletchley Park. Here the codes and cyphers of the German Enigma machine were broken and the intelligence gathered from decoding – known as Ultra – was assessed. It is only relatively recently that historians have fully understood the huge impact of Ultra on the outcome of the war because it gave Britain and its allies access to high-level German secret intelligence without the enemy knowing it.

Myers worked right at the heart of the operation in the legendary Hut 3. He acted as a translator on what was called the Watch, a group of first-class German speakers, many of whom were peacetime schoolteachers, who translated and sifted often incomplete German messages. As Peter Calvocoressi, who also worked in Hut 3, put it, these dozen operators were more than translators because 'they needed to be familiar with the whole intelligence picture in order not to miss a significant clue hidden in the seemingly prosaic message on the scrap of paper before them.'[129]

Three months after she had arrived in Britain following her complex and hazardous journey, Margot Myers moved into a house near Bletchley Park. It was wonderful to be reunited with her husband and to be a family unit once more. But there was still a war going on, and swapping an existence on the family property in occupied France with the relative safety but also banality

[129]Peter Calvocoressi, *Top Secret Ultra* (Cassell, 1980)

of life in England's home counties was not without its pressures.

It was, perhaps, something of an anti-climax after her dramatic escape from German-occupied France. Top Secret Ultra was a demanding master and Myers, conscientious as ever, worked very long hours, sacrificing the family life he had missed so much. Margot understood the desperate importance of the work at Bletchley Park and that losing family time was a sacrifice they needed to make. Yet, unlike most partners, her husband could never discuss his work. Even within Bletchley Park, Hut 3 was isolated and the work was both very complex and extremely secret.

As Calvocoressi rather blandly put it, 'One of the consequences of war is to allow the workplace to usurp many of the hours which a more tranquil dispensation allots to domesticity.'

As his vivid and frank letters show, for Geoffrey Myers being a husband and a father was much more than 'domesticity'. Inevitably, during this period Margot often felt like an outsider, living in an alien environment. News from her family in France was almost non-existent and she was forced to avoid attempting to contact them for fear that her Jewish connection would endanger their lives. She found compensation in her growing children who numbered three when, to great joy, Bernard was born in 1944.

Margot had been lucky to escape the Nazi occupiers. In July 1942, the Nazis arrested more than 13,000 Jews in Paris including over 4,000 children. After being penned like cattle for several days in a velodrome, most, including thousands of children separated from their parents, were transported to Auschwitz.

Torture by the Nazis continued to be commonplace at the local prison in Moulins, La Mal Coiffée. 'They preferably attacked the sexual parts, twisted them with a hand or with a wire, made them grill with a burning newspaper or tore them off with pincers.'[130]

On the exact day in August 1944 that Paris celebrated the surrender of the Nazi garrison, the Germans dragged fifty-six men, nine women and a seven-year-old child from their dungeon in the Gestapo Prison at Moulins, just a few miles from Margot's home. Instead of being liberated, as they should have been under the terms of the German surrender, this mixture of Jews, resistance fighters and the unlucky were bundled onto trains and sent to the concentration camps at Buchenwald and Ravensbrück. Although the war in France was over, only thirty-five of the sixty-six prisoners survived.

Later in the war, Myers worked in 3A, the air intelligence part of Hut 3, as an air advisor. Here his experience at 257 Squadron proved vital. Everyone in 3A had been RAF or USAF officers with experience in the Watch. Now, operating in pairs, they sifted and analysed the material that passed through the Watch before passing the most important and relevant material onwards. Margot knew that she had to support the war effort and her sacrifice was nothing compared to the sacrifices made by the young men whose lives were so dramatically and emotionally described in the letters her husband wrote in his notebook.

Before the war ended, he was elevated to Head of Hut 3, Air Intelligence Section, and is now commemorated on the Codebreakers' Wall. Geoff's work was so secret

[130]Jacky Tronel blog 'Histoire Penitentiaire et Justice Militaire'

he could not even tell his family about it, 'Our lips on our work, called Ultra, were sealed for thirty-five years and nobody in the family knew until recently what I was doing in the last five years of the war.'[131]

After the liberation of Paris, Margot was amazed that her husband, on a mission to Paris, successfully made his way down to Beaurepaire where, Margot recalled, he astonished the locals in Lucenay by escorting his mother-in-law to the village wearing his RAF uniform. But it was not until after the war, in spring 1946, that Margot was able to return home to Beaurepaire herself. She had not seen her mother for nearly five years and it was thrilling to embrace her again. Yet, Margot detected an underlying bitterness in her mother towards some people in the area. Many had been true and kind but others had waited for her mother to fall. 'She had developed a deep resentment towards certain people in her midst. She could see how cowardly they were and how they compromised her principles.' Some locals still thought that, 'The Jews, the communists and the British were responsible for all the misfortunes.'[132]

At the local town hall, Margot was shocked to learn that just after she had escaped a local had denounced her to the Nazis. The Germans who came hunting for Margot and her soon after they escaped had been tipped off by someone the family knew. The officials offered to give her the name of the person who had betrayed her, but Margot decided it was best not to know.

[131]Letter to his grandson, Danny, May 18 1982
[132]Margot Myers memoir, translated by her daughter, Anne

After the war, adjustment to civilian life was difficult for Myers, who had formally left the RAF in 1946 with the rank of Squadron Leader and an MBE. He had lived through the Battle for France, Dunkirk, the Battle of Britain and had been at the heart of the Enigma operation at Bletchley Park. Yet, these experiences and the maturity they brought with them seemed to count for nothing in 1946. It was as if these critical moments in the war, where he had been witness to some of the most significant turning points, had never happened or he had never been there.

Back in Paris, he was taken back on by the *Daily Telegraph* but at the same level he had reached in 1939. He had lost many of his journalistic contacts and some of his pre-war colleagues had overtaken him as a result of successful careers as war correspondents.

His sense of alienation, of difference, was accentuated by having spent seven years in the dark world of secrets and confidential information. Now, back on the journalistic beat, instead of suppressing information he was required to publish it, and instead of accurately weighing up the significance of material, the journalistic need was to often make stories bigger than they really were.

Myers was such a diligent and careful journalist that he slowly overcame this innate conflict within himself and began to shake off the chains of excessive secrecy. He worked hard for the *Daily Telegraph* and when the *Sunday Telegraph* started, he was promoted to be their number-one correspondent. As he admitted, he was happier with the precise requirements of news rather than the features he had to write and he led a successful career for almost all his working life within the Telegraph

Group. His final job, six years before he retired, was as correspondent at the United Nations in New York. It was the ideal job for Myers. It was fresh and exciting and he worked happily there until his retirement at the age of sixty-five. His son Bernard has collated a self-published book of Geoff's journalism.

In retirement he was always on the move, visiting his children in different parts of the world, or looking after his grandchildren while Margot continued to give music lessons in their flat in Paris. The last time I saw him was for lunch in a small French restaurant in Notting Hill Gate in March 1982. He had a huge suitcase that he lumbered about with him because he was on his way to visit his daughter in the USA. After that he was headed back to Beaurepaire, where his wife and children had spent so many agonising months in fear of the Nazis. He was planning to spend the winter there looking after his elderly mother-in-law.

It was typical of Geoffrey's kindness, and also symbolic of his conscientiousness and sense of responsibility, that he had spent the morning at the Public Record Office in Kew double-checking the records of 257 Squadron to ensure that all the information he gave me was accurate. He wrote to me in May 1982 thanking me for the lunch and adding that, having re-examined the squadron records that same morning, 'I knew it would upset me to go through those reports again in detail after more than forty years, but I did not realise that I would also be filled with admiration for what those men accomplished at the time.'[133]

[133]Letter to Author, May 1982

During our warm and friendly meeting, he was twinkly and fun. He confided in me some incidents involving high-profile pilots that he had never told anyone before. 'Someone needs to know,' he kept saying. Having lived with the weight of all that had gone on in one of the most battered squadrons in the Battle of Britain, so much of it secret, it was as if he finally wanted to unburden himself. He was keen that what had been hidden for so long should now be in the open, as any journalist would. He gave me permission to publish his letters and sounded relieved as much as pleased that publication would go ahead.

I should have realised why. Just before our lunch, Myers had been diagnosed with cancer and told he only had a year to live. Of course, his dignity and courage was such that he never told me anything of his illness, and throughout our lunch he was cheerful and convivial.

Myers never had the final year he was promised. Six weeks after our lunch, he died in France, aged seventy-six. His wife, Margot, went on to live to the age of ninety-nine. In 2012 she died in Lexington, Massachusetts, where her daughter, Anne, lives with her family. According to the local obituary Margot continued to teach piano into her late nineties and was known to the family as Mamie Piano. She had nine grandchildren and eleven great-grandchildren. Robert, Anne and Bernard are no longer young, but in good heart, and cherish the extraordinary story of their mother and father.

ACKNOWLEDGMENTS

No book is written in isolation and so I have to thank the many diligent historians and archivists who have recorded the events of the Second World War. Few conflicts have been as comprehensively written about as the Battle of Britain. For *Secret Letters,* the Battle of Britain Monument and Imperial War Museum have been particularly helpful sources as have several books that I have credited.

Thanks also to Janet Willis, whose valuable interviews from the 1980s were found in the loft, still extant, and to those who helped start this enterprise off many years ago including Andy Saunders, Battle of Britain historian, and my colleagues at Yorkshire Television, particularly Peter Moore and Jane Nairac. Special thanks to the late Peter Gordon, whose superb BBC documentary *Missing* first opened the door on 257 Squadron. We later enjoyed working together at Yorkshire.

Miranda Vaughan Jones, supported by Saba Ahmed, has edited the book meticulously and thoughtfully and Philip Beresford created a memorable cover. Tom Willis who did a great job on the promotional videos. My publisher, Richard Charkin, was, as ever, both a wise counsel and good companion and my agent, David Grossman, a diligent supporter.

Yet, of course, the greatest debt of gratitude lies with those who lived through these events of 1939-41 and recorded their thoughts. I was lucky to have met, or been in touch with, several members of 257 squadron back in the 1980s and they are credited in the footnotes. They were, without exception, unfailingly honest and thoughtful about their experiences. Particular thanks to Esther Terry Wright (Terry Hunt) who I met at that time near her flat in Victoria when she was not only fascinating company but agreed that I could use excerpts from her beautifully written book.

However, the deepest thanks must be reserved for Geoff and Margot Myers whose war time experiences, and love for each other and their children, are the rock on which this book is built. Although I have added many other voices, and significant further information into the story in order to amplify what Geoff wrote between 1939-41, without their candour and generosity of spirit there would have been no book.

In addition, I was lucky that Geoff wrote so intuitively and often beautifully about the extraordinary circumstances they both faced. I felt privileged to know them both and to be trusted to tell their astonishing story. If the book has failings, they are of my making not Geoff's.

The kindness of Geoff and Margot was matched by the supportive response of their children. Anne, in Massachusetts, and Bernard, in Paris, willingly provided notes and other vital details. Their brother, Robert, living nearer in the UK, was unfailingly generous and kind both with his time and also with meticulously kept letters and notebooks. Having been handed Geoff's typewritten letters back in 1981 it was remarkable to finally read the originals, written in Geoff's own hand. They are a unique record of an extraordinary period in our history, and the impact that war had on one family who were both ordinary and extraordinary at the same time.

A NOTE ON THE AUTHOR

John Willis, author of *Churchill's Few*, is one of Britain's best known television executives. He is a former director of programmes at Channel 4 and director of factual and learning at the BBC. He was vice-president of national programs at WGBH Boston. In 2012, he was elected as chair of the British Academy of Film and Television Arts (BAFTA).

He is currently chair of Mentorn Media — producers of *Question Time* for BBC — and he also chairs the board of governors at the Royal Central School for Speech and Drama.

He divides his time between London and Norfolk.